CAMPAIGN 312

OPERATION TORCH 1942

The invasion of French North Africa

BRIAN LANE HERDER

ILLUSTRATED BY DARREN TAN
Series editor Marcus Cowper

Osprey Publishing
c/o Bloomsbury Publishing Inc.
1385 Broadway, 5th Floor, New York, NY 10018, USA
E-mail: info@ospreypublishing.com

www.ospreypublishing.com

OSPREY is a trademark of Osprey Publishing Ltd, a division of Bloomsbury Publishing Plc.

First published in Great Britain in 2017.

A CIP catalog record for this book is available from the British Library.

ISBN: Paperback: 978 147282 054 9
        ePub: 978 147282 056 3
        ePDF: 978 147282 055 6
        XML: 978 147282 274 1

17 18 19 20 21   10 9 8 7 6 5 4 3 2 1

Index by Fionbar Lyons
Typeset in Myriad Pro and Sabon
Maps by Bounford.com
3D BEVs by The Black Spot
Page layouts by PDQ Digital Media Solutions, Bungay, UK
Printed in China through World Print Ltd.

Osprey Publishing supports the Woodland Trust, the UK's leading woodland conservation charity. Between 2014 and 2018 our donations are being spent on their Centenary Woods project in the UK.

To find out more about our authors and books visit
www.ospreypublishing.com. Here you will find extracts, author interviews, details of forthcoming events and the option to sign up for our newsletter.

ACKNOWLEDGMENTS

I would like to thank Geoff Slee at www.combinedops.com for the photo of HMS *Misoa*, and also Mike Kemble at www.captainwalker.uk for the photo of the Algiers waterfront. Additionally, I would like to thank Mike Fraticelli at www.ww2survivorstories.com, whose father Anthony L. Fraticelli was a US Coast Guardsman aboard transport USS *Thomas Stone* during Operation *Torch*. Mr Fraticelli found for me the NARA photo of 33rd FG departing USS *Chenango* and graciously shared his fascinating research on the *Thomas Stone*'s November 7, 1942 torpedoing. Finally, I would like to thank the Osprey Publishing staff for giving me the chance to publish the book I always wanted to read, and editors Marcus Cowper and Nikolai Bogdanovic for their support and guidance through the publishing process.

IMAGE CREDITS

Combined Operations	www.combinedops.com
Critical Past	www.criticalpast.com
Getty Images	www.gettyimages.co.uk
LOC	Library of Congress (www.loc.gov)
NARA	National Archives and Records Administration (www.archives.gov)
Navsource	NavSource Naval History (www.navsource.org)
Wikimedia Commons	https://commons.wikimedia.org
World War II Database	ww2db.com
World War II Today	ww2today.com

Imperial War Museums Collections
Many of the photos in this book come from the huge collections of IWM (Imperial War Museums) which cover all aspects of conflict involving Britain and the Commonwealth since the start of the 20th century. These rich resources are available online to search, browse and buy at www.iwm.org. uk/collections. In addition to Collections Online, you can visit the Visitor Rooms where you can explore over 8 million photographs, thousands of hours of moving images, the largest sound archive of its kind in the world, thousands of diaries and letters written by people in wartime, and a huge reference library. To make an appointment, call (020) 7416 5320, or e-mail mail@iwm.org.uk.
www.iwm.org.uk

DEDICATION

This first book is dedicated to the love of my life, Evelyn Rose Herder, who helped Daddy "color" the original Longstop Hill map when she was 4 years old. May your life be more peaceful than the events depicted here.

Key to military symbols

Army Group, Army, Corps, Division, Brigade, Regiment, Battalion, Company/Battery, Platoon, Section, Squad, Infantry, Artillery, Cavalry, Airborne, Unit HQ, Air defense, Air Force, Air mobile, Air transportable, Amphibious, Antitank, Armor, Air aviation, Bridging, Engineer, Headquarters, Maintenance, Medical, Missile, Mountain, Navy, Nuclear, biological, chemical, Ordnance, Parachute, Reconnaissance, Signal, Supply, Transport movement, Rocket artillery, Air defense artillery

Key to unit identification

Unit identifier, Parent unit, Commander, (+) with added elements, (–) less elements

CONTENTS

Operation *Torch*, October 21–December 25, 1942.

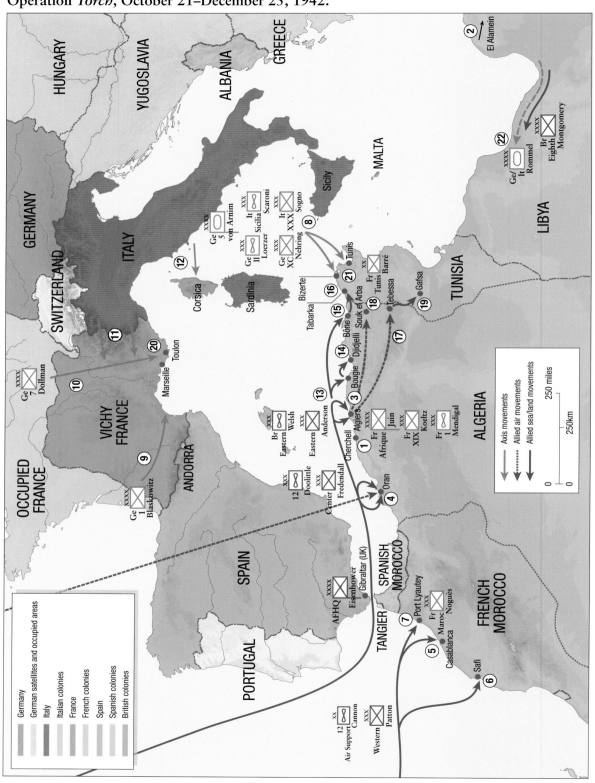

ORIGINS OF THE CAMPAIGN

VICHY FRANCE 1940–41

On June 22, 1940, Nazi Germany formalized its rapid victory over France with the Armistice of Compiègne. The Wehrmacht was to militarily occupy three-fifths of the country, including Paris and the Channel and Atlantic coasts. The French government would maintain civil administration of the nation, though subject to German direction in the occupied zone. The French army in metropolitan France, to be known as the Armée de l'Armistice, was confined to the unoccupied *zone libre* in southeast France, stripped of heavy weapons, and restricted to a strength of 94,200. The Gendarmerie was limited to 60,000, plus a 10,000-strong antiaircraft corps.

Germany abstained from confiscating the French fleet or colonies. France would keep both under conditions of strict neutrality, monitored and enforced by the Axis. France was allowed to keep 150,000 men under arms to defend its overseas empire against foreign incursion: 55,000 in Morocco, 50,000 in Algeria, and 40,000 in the Armée du Levant (Lebanon and Syria). The Compiègne terms were not as severe as the Allies' later "unconditional surrender" imposed on Germany and Japan. The Nazis were motivated to quickly and cleanly conclude hostilities in the West to prepare for Hitler's showdown with the Soviet Union. More crushing terms may have driven the French to continue fighting at home and overseas. As it was, the Armistice of Compiègne offered the French an illusion of maintaining national sovereignty.

Germany's refusal to claim the powerful French surface fleet was partially intended to mollify the British but this gesture failed. British national security depended on control of the sea and French promises to never surrender the Marine Nationale to Germany were insufficient. On July 3, 1940 Churchill regretfully ordered the Royal Navy's Force H to destroy a major part of the French fleet at Mers-el-Kébir. The French government was outraged at the apparent treachery and severed relations with Britain.

The following week, on July 10, France's National Assembly convened at the unoccupied spa town of Vichy to ratify the Compiègne armistice. Additionally the National Assembly voted by 569 to 80 to amend the French constitution and effectively confer dictatorial powers to new premier Phillipe Pétain. The following day, Pétain dissolved the Third Republic (*République française*), and replaced it with a new far-right national government, the French State (*État français*).

1. Cherchell Conference, October 21–22, 1942.
2. Second battle of El Alamein (in Egypt), October 23–November 11, 1942.
3. Landings at Algiers, November 8, 1942.
4. Landings at Oran, November 8–10, 1942.
5. Landings at Fedala/Casablanca, November 8–11, 1942.
6. Landings at Safi, November 8–10, 1942.
7. Landings at Port Lyautey, November 8–10, 1942.
8. Axis begin landing at Tunisia, November 9, 1942.
9. *Case Anton* (German 1. Armee), November 11, 1942.
10. *Case Anton* (German 7.Armee), November 11, 1942.
11. *Case Anton* (Italian occupation of southeast France), November 11, 1942.
12. *Case Anton* (Italian occupation of Corsica), November 11, 1942.
13. British First Army's 36th Brigade Group lands at Bougie, November 11, 1942.
14. British 36th Brigade Group lands at Djidjelli, November 12, 1942.
15. British 3rd Battalion, Parachute Regiment and No. 6 Commando occupy Bône, November 12, 1942.
16. Advance elements of 36th Brigade Group occupy Tabarka, November 15, 1942.
17. US 2nd/509th Parachute Infantry Regiment occupies Youks-les-Bains Airfield and Tébessa, November 15, 1942.
18. British 1st Battalion, Parachute Regiment drops on Souk el Arba, November 16, 1942.
19. US 2nd/509th Parachute Infantry Regiment occupies Gafsa, November 22, 1942.
20. Operation *Lila*, scuttling of the French fleet at Toulon, November 27, 1942.
21. Main Tunisian campaign, November 25–December 25, 1942.
22. Western Desert front movements, December 25, 1942.

Philippe Pétain shakes hands with Adolf Hitler in June 1940. Pétain's Vichy regime attracted disaffected right-wing elements, often ardent Catholics and various conservatives who had felt marginalized in republican France. They viewed temporary collaboration with the Nazis as a lesser evil to French society than internal decay from liberals, atheists, and Communists. (IWM HU 076027)

The United States did not sever relations with Vichy France, instead considering diplomatic and economic pressure the most pragmatic means to keep Vichy from allying with Nazi Germany. In December 1940, Roosevelt sent talented diplomat Robert Murphy to Algiers to negotiate an economic assistance program to French North Africa – the "carrot" in the carrot-and-stick American diplomacy to Vichy. The resulting Murphy-Weygand trade accord was signed February 26, 1941. By December 1941, the assistance program to French North Africa appeared highly successful. US officials had established a human network on the ground and American influence in the region appeared to have greatly expanded.

ANGLO-AMERICAN GRAND STRATEGY 1941–42

The British and US joint chiefs of staff had secretly discussed grand strategy against the Axis throughout 1941. Upon the United States' official entry into the war, the relationship between Britain and the United States became an

Mers-el-Kébir, Algeria, July 3, 1940. After prolonged negotiations failed, Admiral James Somerville ordered the Royal Navy's Force H to execute Operation *Catapult*, the destruction of the French battle fleet. When it was over, 1,297 French sailors were dead. Somerville admitted, "We all feel thoroughly ashamed." Facing invasion, his country widely approved the action. (NARA)

open alliance. Of concern was how to best coordinate British and American forces, and how to most efficiently employ the United States' latent war-making power against the Axis. The first wartime conference, Arcadia, convened December 22, 1941. To British relief Roosevelt and the US joint chiefs reaffirmed the strategic policy of "Europe first." Additionally, US Army Chief of Staff George C. Marshall proposed each theater be under a unified command, and the US joint staff and British joint staff organized into the Combined Chiefs of Staff.

Before Pearl Harbor, both nations had considered the employment of forces against Vichy French colonies. In January 1941, the US had developed *Barrister*, a plan for a pre-emptive invasion of Dakar, seen as a potential Wehrmacht staging base against the Western Hemisphere. The British proposed strong landings in French North Africa as a way to break the deadlock of the Western Desert campaign. On December 26, 1941 Anglo-American planners presented a tentative study of "The North African Project." A British landing in the Mediterranean was dubbed *Gymnast*; when combined with earlier US plans to land on the Moroccan coast, it became *Super-Gymnast*. Allied planners labored under severe global shipping shortages which hamstrung force size. Planners hoped that local French authorities would issue an "invitation" to the Allies to occupy French North Africa, but this was not forthcoming. By February 1942, conditions in North Africa and the Pacific had deteriorated and *Super-Gymnast* was shelved.

In Moscow, Stalin was insistent the Western Allies launch a second front in 1942 to relieve the Soviets. His assertion was shared by Roosevelt, who remarked: "It must be reminded the Russian armies are killing more Germans and destroying more Axis materiel than all of the other twenty-five United Nations put together." American planners, indoctrinated with Halford Mackinder's 1904 "Heartland Theory," regarded a Soviet collapse as a global catastrophe, a view not shared so strongly by the British. As the Allies' worldwide situation deteriorated, the US staff rallied around the most direct possible strategy against Nazi Germany – unleashing overwhelming land and air power from Britain against Germany itself, the strategic *Schwerpunkt*. Drawing partly from US plans for a 1942 invasion of Europe and British plans for a conditional 1943 invasion, the US staff presented the Marshall Memorandum to the British joint chiefs on April 8, 1942.

The Marshall Memorandum proposed three complementary operations. The first was *Bolero*, an enormous transatlantic movement of US troops and materiel to Great Britain, to eventually reach 1 million US service personnel by spring 1943. *Bolero* would precede the second operation, *Roundup*, a cross-Channel invasion of the Continent by 48 divisions and 5,800 aircraft, to be launched by April 1, 1943. The third operation was *Sledgehammer*, a much smaller landing on the Continent in 1942. *Sledgehammer* was a contingency invasion that would be undertaken if circumstances appeared unusually favorable or desperate. In the event the Soviet Union appeared on the verge of collapse in 1942, *Sledgehammer* would become an emergency cross-Channel attack of one British division, a British airborne brigade, and three American airborne battalions no later than September 15.[1] Ideally a lodgment would be established at Le Havre, which would be defended by aggressive RAF air cover over the winter and built up to eight divisions (six

---

1 *Sledgehammer* was as much an evolving concept as it was a developed plan. Specific details are sparse and vary greatly depending on source/date.

The wartime US joint chiefs of staff, 1943. From left to right, General Henry "Hap" Arnold (USAAF), Admiral William D. Leahy (US Navy, chairman), Admiral Ernest J. King (US Navy), and General George C. Marshall (US Army). These talented men early on "had our shirts handed to us" by their well-organized British counterparts. But at Tehran, in November 1943, the American delegation cleverly trapped a grumpy Churchill into firmly committing to *Overlord*. (US Navy)

British, two American) by spring 1943. Optimistically, German divisions would be withdrawn from the Eastern Front to deal with the threat and the Luftwaffe lured into a battle of destruction over the bridgehead.

The British formally accepted the full Marshall Memorandum on April 14. Therefore *Bolero* was commenced, *Roundup* a firm expectation for 1943, and *Sledgehammer* an option for 1942.[2] The US staff appeared to have gotten their way. Yet Churchill never abandoned French North Africa, cheerfully reminding his allies, "We must never forget *Gymnast*." Roosevelt too remained highly interested in the region because of the Murphy-Weygand accord; the President was not later a naïve tool of Churchill's manipulation as often portrayed.

In early June 1942, the US Navy won a smashing victory at Midway. With the West Coast secure, air and ground units were freed from North American defense and available for the European theater. In Britain the Americans began to assemble the administrative machinery to execute *Bolero* and *Sledgehammer–Roundup*. On June 8, 1942 the European Theater of Operations, US Army (ETOUSA) was organized, with Marshall naming his favorite new protégé Major-General Dwight D. Eisenhower as commander. On June 15, the headquarters of the US Army Air Forces (USAAF) in Britain, the Eighth Air Force, was established outside London.

However, the British were becoming increasingly vocal with concerns about *Sledgehammer*, starting with landing craft. At least 8,100 landing craft were needed by September. Unexpected delays in the construction program meant only 4,000 were expected, and British planners believed most of these were too small and unseaworthy for the Channel. The plan had always been risky and the British had most to lose in a 1942 assault. By June, British enthusiasm for *Sledgehammer*, if it had ever existed, was evaporating. Churchill stressed a premature invasion would be disastrous, noting, "Wars are not won by unsuccessful operations."

On July 8, 1942 the British informed the Americans that *Sledgehammer* was out of the question. The Americans were aware no European operation could be undertaken without full British support. They believed the *Sledgehammer* veto implied the British were wavering on the entire Marshall Memorandum. Perturbed, Marshall lobbied Roosevelt to force the issue with an ultimatum that the British support the complete plan or else the US would go "full-out in the Pacific." Roosevelt asked Marshall what plans existed for a Pacific first strategy. There were none. It was a bluff and Roosevelt had called it – the President had no intention of abandoning "Europe first."

2 Until mid-1942, Allied codename usage was imprecise. *Gymnast* variously meant British Mediterranean landings, US Moroccan landings, or (usually) *Super-Gymnast*. *Sledgehammer* and *Roundup* were often reversed. *Bolero* sometimes implied *Roundup*.

Unlike his military chiefs, Roosevelt's strategic outlook was influenced by domestic politics – a factor Marshall later admitted had escaped him at the time. Pearl Harbor had enraged the American public against Japan, not Germany. Therefore, Roosevelt was adamant that the United States be committed to a major operation against Germany in 1942, before inflamed American opinion forced the main effort to be irretrievably cast against Japan.

Roosevelt sent the US staff back to London with instructions to lobby hard for *Sledgehammer*, but under no circumstances were they to return without an absolute decision for a 1942 offensive. The US delegation again failed to persuade the British on *Sledgehammer*, conceding defeat on July 22. Roosevelt authorized his staff to consider five alternative operations for 1942:

1. *Super-Gymnast*, a combined invasion of French North Africa
2. *Gymnast*, an American-only invasion of French Morocco
3. *Jupiter*, a combined invasion of northern Norway
4. An American reinforcement of Egypt
5. An American reinforcement of Iran

On July 24, the US staff proposed *Super-Gymnast* as the least-objectionable alternative for 1942, while noting this made *Roundup*, the planned 1943 invasion of Europe, unlikely. The British accepted and the combined North Africa operation was renamed *Torch*. The Combined Chiefs decreed *Torch*'s commander be American and included another concession: of 1,500 US aircraft earmarked for Britain, some 700 were to be diverted to North Africa; the remaining 800 were to reinforce the Pacific. *Sledgehammer* was officially canceled. The new agreements were outlined in the memorandum CCS 94, "Operations in 1942–43" and transmitted to Roosevelt on July 25. Churchill was delighted, slyly informing Roosevelt, "I am your ardent lieutenant in this enterprise."

Operation *Torch*'s political goals were to secure outlying French colonies against the Axis and to engage the United States in ground combat against Germany and Italy in 1942. The strategic objectives were to divert Wehrmacht forces from the Eastern Front, to trap and destroy the Axis' armies in North Africa, to eliminate the threat of the French Navy joining the Germans, and to reclaim the Mediterranean as Britain's primary convoy route with its eastern empire.

Operation *Torch* is remarkable for decisively sidelining *Bolero* and *Roundup*. *Torch* was neither a strategic sideshow to the ETO, nor a scheduled warm-up match for an inevitable future invasion of Northwest Europe. In November 1942, it was the primary Anglo-American offensive for the foreseeable future; no other major campaigns were planned. Between August 1942 and December 1942, US military shipments to Britain fell from 800,000 ship tons per month to 100,000 ship tons. US personnel strength in Britain peaked at 228,000 in October 1942, dropped to 135,000 by late December, and bottomed out at 105,000 by February 1943. By then a total of 156,000 US personnel had been withdrawn from Britain.

THE SHIPS ARE COMING

UNITED STATES SHIPPING BOARD ▪ EMERGENCY FLEET CORPORATION

Unprepared for the severe shipping shortage of World War I, the United States government had undertaken a crash shipbuilding program, illustrated by this 1917 Emergency Fleet Corporation poster. Between 1920 and 1941, this huge war-built merchant fleet of 9.9 million tons had been allowed to decline to just 3 million tons, forcing history to repeat itself. Lack of shipping dominated Allied strategic planning in 1942. (LOC)

OPERATION *TORCH* TAKES SHAPE, JULY 25–NOVEMBER 7, 1942

Administration, manpower, and materiel for *Torch* – mostly American – were simply plundered from *Bolero*. In August 1942, Allied Force Headquarters, North Africa (AFHQ), was established in London. Eisenhower, who had privately referred to the *Torch* decision as "the blackest day in history," was named commander. Most air power for the North African theater would be provided by the new US Twelfth Air Force, established August 20, 1942. Its aircraft, personnel, and staff were largely cannibalized by gutting Eighth Air Force in Britain, earning Twelfth Air Force the nickname "Eighth Air Force Junior."

In England, Eisenhower admirably assembled a truly integrated Anglo-American staff. Planning began immediately but was hampered by micromanagement from Washington and London. Eisenhower, irritated, referred to a "transatlantic essay contest." *Torch* couldn't help but be ridden with compromises. A worldwide shipping shortage dictated a maximum of three major landings. Eisenhower and the British deemed the early occupation of Tunisia the overriding objective, desiring all three landings in the Mediterranean with the most easterly landing at Bône. Washington-bound US staff feared Franco's neutral but Nazi-friendly Spain might close the Straits of Gibraltar, resulting in strategic disaster. For absolute security, Washington planners insisted on an Atlantic landing in French Morocco, a thousand miles to the rear. The British considered Morocco irrelevant but were in no position to veto the Americans again.

The final plan involved three invasion forces. The Eastern and Center Task Forces staging from Britain would land in Algeria at Algiers and Oran. The Western Task Force staging from the United States would land in French Morocco at Casablanca. Setting D-Day was problematic. Strategic surprise and the urgency of the Eastern Front were best served by the earliest possible landing date, yet planning, the conversion of civilian liners into combat loaders, and the necessity of training demanded extra time. D-Day was postponed multiple times and finally set to midnight November 8.[3] AFHQ feared winter sea conditions would make landings much later impossible. Additionally, planners assumed the French would be hostile to the British and went to extravagant lengths to conceal British involvement, instead presenting the landings as an all-American operation.

On October 16, the US War Department sent an electrifying telegram to AFHQ in London. US high consul and master spy Robert Murphy (alias Colonel McGowan) requested a top-secret conference in Algeria. A genuine cloak-and-dagger mission – Operation *Flagpole* –

Norfolk Naval Station, October 21, 1942: 77 P-40s of the USAAF's 33rd Fighter Group are loaded aboard auxiliary aircraft carrier USS *Chenango* for Operation *Torch*. Western Task Force elements sortied from multiple East Coast ports and then made a perfect mid-Atlantic rendezvous on October 28. The next stop was Morocco, where Patton's stated intentions were to "conquer … or be destroyed." (Navsource)

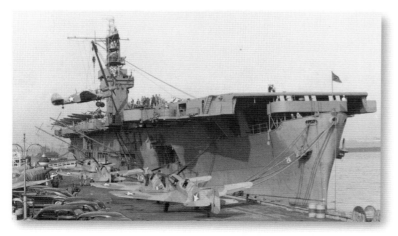

3   Roosevelt preferred D-Day predate the November 3, 1942 Congressional elections, but never pressured *Torch* planners. The President's Democratic party lost seats, but retained majorities of 57 to 39 in the Senate and 222 to 213 in the House.

was arranged. Royal Navy submarine HMS *Seraph* surfaced off the shore of Cherchell, Algeria on the night of October 21/22. Led by *Torch* deputy commander Major-General Mark Clark, a small high-ranking US party was rowed ashore, escorted by a bodyguard of British commandos. Murphy conducted them to a friend's villa. The French commander-in-chief in Algiers, Général Charles Mast, arrived at dawn and parlayed with the Allies. Mast explained the French army might defect to the Allies if led by French Général Henri Giraud. That afternoon, acting on a tip, a surprise police raid nearly bagged the entire group.[4] Clark and his compatriots fled before returning safely to *Seraph* that night.

Torch would be a huge and complex operation, prepared hurriedly and with limited resources, and requiring the intimate cooperation of brand-new allies. American and British efforts to pull off *Torch* were therefore quite impressive. In September, units of the Western Task Force had been assigned to the Amphibious Force, Atlantic Fleet in Virginia to train for ship-to-shore amphibious assault. Center and Eastern Task Force units trained in Britain. Bound for North Africa, all three task forces quietly departed the United States and Britain between October 22 and 26. Upon receiving the news, Roosevelt mused, "At last we are on our way." Although not directly coordinated with *Torch*, on October 23, Montgomery had opened his long-awaited offensive at El Alamein and by early November it was clear Eighth Army had won a huge victory. *Torch* was now poised to strike the Axis' retreating North African armies in the rear. On the night of November 5/6, transports of the Center and Eastern Task Forces slipped through the Straits of Gibraltar. The Germans were aware Allied ships had entered the Mediterranean, but were uncertain of their purpose or destination.

That same night HMS *Seraph* – disguised as American – surfaced off unoccupied France to execute Operation *Kingpin*. On the beach waited eccentric French Général Henri Giraud, who had escaped house arrest in Lyon. Weeks earlier, AFHQ had secretly offered Giraud command of all French forces in Africa. *Seraph* spirited the general aboard and Giraud arrived at Gibraltar on the afternoon of November 7. Upon arrival, Giraud calmly explained he expected to be commander-in-chief of the entire Allied invasion and would accept no subordinate position. Eisenhower was dumbfounded. The Americans pleaded for Giraud to accept the original offer. The French general made a final refusal: "Giraud will remain a spectator in this affair."

A North Africa-bound transport takes on combat equipment at Merseyside, UK in November 1942. The date suggests this was part of a convoy following the initial assault force, as the last invasion transport had sailed October 26. (IWM H025021)

Clark placed him under arrest and AFHQ sent a signal in French from "Giraud" informing Mast that Giraud was working for the Allies. History's greatest amphibious invasion to date loomed mere hours away. American historian Samuel E. Morison aptly recalled Thucydides when documenting his account of Operation *Torch*. In 413 BC, Nicias, commander of the ill-fated Syracuse expedition, had addressed the Athenian assembly before departure: "We are like men going to found a city in a land of strangers and enemies, who on the very day of their disembarkation must have command of the country; for if they meet with a disaster, they will have no friends."

4 Clark and his men hid in a wine cellar for hours, sidearms drawn. Above them Murphy feigned drunkenness and schmoozed the police until Clark's party could bolt and hide in the coastal sand dunes until dark.

CHRONOLOGY

1940

June 22 — Compiègne Armistice signed.

July 3 — British attack French at Mers-el-Kébir. France severs relations with Britain.

July 11 — Pétain dissolves French Third Republic, replaces it with French State (Vichy France).

1941

February 26 — Murphy-Weygand accord signed.

December 11 — Germany declares war on the United States.

December 22 — Arcadia Conference convenes.

1942

April 14 — British accept Marshall Memorandum.

July 8 — British renege on *Sledgehammer*.

July 24 — Combined Chiefs agree to undertake *Torch*.

October 21–22 — Cherchell Conference.

October 23 — Montgomery opens El Alamein offensive.

November 8 — *Torch* D-Day. Three Allied task forces land in Algeria and French Morocco. France severs relations with United States. Algiers surrenders.

November 9 — Germans begin landing in Tunisia.

November 10 — Oran surrenders. Allies begin negotiations with Darlan. First Allied convoy departs Algiers for Tunisian offensive.

November 11 — Casablanca surrenders. Axis' *Case Anton* overruns unoccupied France.

November 17 — General Nehring takes command of Axis XC Korps in Tunis. Allies and Axis first clash at Djebel Abiod.

November 19 — German ultimatum to Tunisian French expires; Germans open battle at Medjez el Bab.

November 22 — Clark–Darlan Agreement concluded. French West Africa defects to Darlan.

November 25 — Allies open set-piece offensive against Axis in Tunisia.

December 1 — German counteroffensive begins.

December 22 — Allies resume Tunis drive at Longstop Hill.

December 24 — AFHQ cancels Tunisian offensive for 1942; *Torch* officially ends. Darlan is assassinated.

1943

January 20 — Rommel orders Deutsch-Italienische Panzerarmee to retreat from Libya to Tunisia.

February 14 — Major Tunisian hostilities resume as Germans launch Operation *Frühlingswind*.

February 19–25 — Battle of Kasserine Pass. Allied shake-up follows.

May 13 — Last Axis forces in North Africa surrender. Original *Torch* mission completed.

OPPOSING COMMANDERS

ALLIED

Torch was the first campaign against Germany employing Marshall's concept of unified theater command. Allied Force[5] was led by an American commander-in-chief assisted by British lieutenants (deputy, naval, and air commanders). Individual officers were allowed to directly appeal to their respective national military establishments only under strict conditions "of the gravest emergency." Allied Force was essentially identical to the theater command of a single nation. The Allies retained this highly successful format through 1945.

British and American elements often integrated. Cultural friction was real but exaggerated. The British generally considered Americans enthusiastic, but military amateurs, while many American officers were outright Anglophobes. American command culture was less centralized, placing comparatively higher value on subordinate initiative; British command style was much more precise and detailed. When commanded by British superiors, American

5 Allied Force was originally dubbed Allied Expeditionary Force. Eisenhower renamed it for security reasons.

Operation *Torch*'s four biggest players in Algiers, November 13, 1942. From left to right: Eisenhower, Darlan, Clark, and Murphy. The latter's extraordinary 61-year US government career began with the Post Office in 1916 and ended in 1977 as a Presidential advisor. For his part in *Torch*, Murphy was awarded the Distinguished Service Medal. (US Army)

Western Task Force commanders Major-General George S. Patton (left) and Rear Admiral Henry "Kent" Hewitt (right) share a laugh aboard the flagship USS *Augusta*. After Patton's initial frostiness, the outspoken general and reserved admiral forged an excellent working relationship as their combined staffs hammered out details of the Morocco invasion. (World War II Database)

subordinates often perceived micromanagement and lack of confidence. Overall, however, Allied command arrangements functioned surprisingly well and would improve with time.

Roosevelt named newly promoted **Lieutenant-General Dwight D. Eisenhower** commander-in-chief. An affable, unassuming Kansan, Eisenhower would reveal great skill and tact in assembling and maintaining a multi-national alliance. The British were initially unimpressed by Eisenhower; Chief of the Imperial General Staff Alan Brooke later remarked, "If I had been told then of the future that lay in front of him, I should have refused to believe it." British officers eventually requested an American deputy commander to preserve *Torch*'s "all-American" façade. Eisenhower selected youthful **Major-General Mark Clark**. AFHQ's naval and air chiefs were **Admiral Sir Andrew Cunningham** and **Air Commodore A. P. H. Saunders**.

Eastern Task Force's naval command fell under **Vice-Admiral Harold Burrough** (RN). To conceal British involvement, **Major-General Charles Ryder** (US) commanded Algiers' assault landings. After D-Day, ground forces and the ensuing "Race for Tunis" would be commanded by **Lieutenant-General Kenneth Anderson**, a stereotypically dour Scot to whom AFHQ assigned the radio call sign "Grouch." Naturally cautious and introspective, Anderson admitted to "a queer sort of shyness" that inhibited him socially.

Commodore Thomas Troubridge (RN) commanded Center Task Force's naval flotilla. **Major-General Lloyd Fredendall** (US) was in charge of Center Task Force's ground forces, but Oran operations were essentially conducted by US 1st Infantry Division commander **Major-General Terry de la Mesa Allen**

and his near-mirror image deputy, **Brigadier-General Teddy Roosevelt, Jr**, son of the 26th President. Ragged in decorum, Allen and Roosevelt were incorrigible fighters and would mold "The Big Red One" into the US Army's most celebrated wartime division.

Calm and thoughtful, **Rear Admiral Henry "Kent" Hewitt** (US) commanded Western Task Force's naval elements. Hewitt would eventually direct every US Atlantic theater landing save Normandy; by 1945 no American better claimed the Mediterranean's ancient sobriquet *mare nostrum*. Hewitt's US Army counterpart was melodramatic **Major-General George S. Patton**. Better remembered for later campaigns, *Torch* highlighted Patton's overlooked skills for amphibious operations, diplomacy, and occupation. Patton's Mehdia–Port Lyautey landings were led by **Major-General Lucian Truscott**, while 2nd Armored Division's **Major-General Ernest Harmon** directed the Safi operation.

Once established in North Africa, Allied land-based theater airpower would fall under Eastern Air Command's **Air Marshal Sir William Welsh** (RAF) and Western Air Command's **Major-General James Doolittle** (USAAF).

AFHQ recruited **Général Henri Giraud** to command pro-Allied French forces. Physically courageous but personally bizarre, Giraud's greatest talent was making dramatic escapes from German prisons in both World Wars. His primary appeal to the Allies was his four-star rank and well-known hostility to the Vichy and Nazi regimes.

FRENCH

French officers' loyalty to the Vichy regime varied. The Nazis were generally disliked to despised, but seemingly non-stop British and American military disasters hardly inspired confidence in defying the Wehrmacht.

Vichy's military commander-in-chief was **Amiral de la flotte Jean-François Darlan**, a notorious Nazi collaborator and well hated by the British and American publics. Darlan praised Nazi military prowess but privately disapproved of its racial policies. In 1941, he had been Pétain's deputy but by May 1942, Darlan's favor had waned. He had begun secretly negotiating with the Americans, claiming that an Allied invasion of 50,000 would be fought, but that of 500,000 would be welcomed. Above all Darlan was an opportunist.

Général de corps Alphonse Juin commanded Vichy's Armée d'Afrique and exercised operational control of North Africa's Armée de l'Air assets. His top commander was **Général de corps Louis-Marie Koeltz**. The Division d'Algers' **Général de division Charles Mast** was Algeria's highest-ranking Allied conspirator.

Général Charles Noguès was Resident-General of Morocco. Once ardently anti-Vichy, his faith in Allied intervention had collapsed and the Allies nicknamed him "No–Yes" for his wavering. **Général de division Émile Béthouart** of the Casablanca Division was the top Allied conspirator in Morocco.

In Tunisia, **Vice-Amiral Jean-Pierre Estéva** was Resident-General and **Général de division Georges Barré** Tunisian army commander. Barré had long considered an Axis invasion of Tunisia inevitable and had secretly stockpiled military caches in the Tunisian hinterlands for just this scenario.

North Africa's anti-Vichy Resistance was loosely coordinated by the Committee of Five, who had conducted the Cherchell Conference and originally recruited Giraud. The Resistance's most significant cell, at Algiers, was led by local Jews **José Aboulker** and **Bernard Karsenty**.

AXIS

Unlike the Allies, the Axis possessed no unified theater command in the Mediterranean. Theoretically, Mussolini was in charge; realistically, the Italians submitted to German direction, while each Wehrmacht branch independently maintained its own Rome headquarters.

Luftwaffe Generalfeldmarschall Albert Kesselring of Oberbefehlshaber (OB) Süd commanded all the Mediterranean and Aegean coastline directly held by German troops with the exception of Rommel's forces. An artillery officer in World War I, Kesselring learned to fly at 48 and had been part of the secret German air force rearmament; he was officially transferred to the Luftwaffe in 1933. Kesselring then commanded Luftlotte 2 during the campaigns against France, Britain, and the Soviet Union before being transferred to Italy in November 1941. Known as "Smiling Al" for his upbeat personality, Kesselring had an uncanny ability to predict his enemies' actions and would prove one of Germany's top theater commanders.

Arriving first in Tunisia was II Fliegerkorps commander **General der Flieger Bruno Loerzer**, whose bold and decisive action would seize the initiative for Germany. Initial German command in Tunisia was XC Korps under the former Afrika Korps commander, **General der Panzertruppen Walther Nehring**. Nehring never fully impressed his superiors. Dissatisfied with Nehring's leadership, on December 9, Hitler established above XC Korps the 5.Panzer-Armee, to be led by **Generaloberst Hans-Jürgen von Arnim**. The latter would eventually replace Rommel as commander Heeresgruppe Afrika in March 1943, just in time to be captured by the Allies. Throughout *Torch*, the Axis' most dynamic Tunisian field officer was the 10.Panzer-Division commander, hyper aggressive **Generalmajor Wolfgang Fischer**.

Generale di Corpo d'Armata Vittorio Sogno would command Italian forces in Tunisia. Italian faith in their ally was badly shaken by El Alamein. Neither the Axis' Mediterranean command arrangements nor German-Italian relations ever functioned so well as Allied Force.

Capable and aggressive, the 53-year-old von Arnim was a textbook Prussian field officer from a family boasting an illustrious military tradition. When he and Heeresgruppe Afrika were forced to surrender in May 1943, Allied officers universally found him a bitter and sullen character. Eisenhower refused to meet him. Von Arnim is seen here three days after his capture. (US Army)

OPPOSING FORCES

ALLIED

D-Day strength of the combined three Task Forces afloat came to 107 transports, 107,453 troops, 9,911 vehicles, and 96,089 tons of supplies. By December 1, 253,213 Allied troops would be ashore. Britain provided most naval power; the United States most land and air power.

The Royal Navy conducted the Algiers and Oran landings, briefly leaving global responsibilities undefended to project significant power inside the Mediterranean for *Torch*. British warships were attached to each of the Eastern and Center Task Forces. Supporting both task forces was Gibraltar's powerful Force H. Altogether the Royal Navy wielded six aircraft carriers, two battleships, one battlecruiser, one monitor, nine cruisers, and scores of escorts and specialized supporting vessels. In quality and professionalism, the Royal Navy of 1942 was still unsurpassed.

The US Navy conducted the Western Task Force off Morocco as Task Force 34, which included five carriers, three battleships, seven cruisers, and the usual escorts. American ships were overwhelmingly manned by reservists and new recruits going to sea for the first time. American landing craft crews were often badly inexperienced in basic seamanship. US naval aviators were highly trained, flying outdated F4F Wildcat fighters but solid SBD Dauntless and TBF Avenger bombers.

Most Allied transports and cargo ships were crash conversions from civilian passenger liners and freighters. British amphibious doctrine dictated the Algiers and Oran landings and American doctrine at Morocco. The RAF provided air support parties for Center and Eastern Task Forces, while the Royal Navy manned landing craft and beach parties. Unlike the Americans, the British brought their transports as close to shore as possible, considering rapid unloading worth the great danger from hostile fire. Large British assault transports were designated LSI(L)s; their American counterparts were called "combat loaders" (eventually designated "attack transports"). An average combat loader carried around 2,000 troops, 2,200

SBD-3 Dauntlesses of VGS-26 and F4F-4 Wildcats of VGF-26 spotted aboard the auxiliary aircraft carrier USS *Sangamon* (ACV-26) during Operation *Torch*, November 1942. *Sangamon* and her type were originally designated AVGs (Aircraft Escort Vessels), then reclassified ACVs (Auxiliary Aircraft Carrier) on August 20, 1942. They would not receive the better-remembered CVE designation (Escort Aircraft Carrier) until July 15, 1943. (Navsource)

Designed to ship petroleum through Venezuela's Lake Maracaibo, the shallow-draft British tankers *Misoa*, *Tasajera*, and *Bachaquero* were requisitioned by the Royal Navy and refitted into the first LSTs in 1941. Displacing 4,200 tons, each could land 20 light tanks directly onto the beach. *Misoa* is seen here in her late 1930s civilian configuration. (Combined Operations)

An M7 Priest lands at Morocco, November 9, 1942. The Priest received its nickname from the raised "pulpit" that mounted its .50-cal. heavy machine gun. The M7 quickly became the US armored divisions' standard self-propelled artillery for the rest of the war. (US Army)

tons of equipment, and 20 integral landing craft deployed via davits. Primary landing craft used in *Torch* were British LCAs and American LCPRs and LCVs. Tank lighters were mostly LCM(3)s although the Americans used some LCM(2)s at Morocco. A handful of early LVT "amtraks" appeared in a logistical role. DUKWs and purpose-built LSTs were unavailable for *Torch*, having just begun mass-production. Specialized ships were requisitioned from civilian service such as seatrain USS *Lakehurst*, the three "Maracaibo" tankers (proto-LSTs), and freighter SS *Contessa*.

Eastern Task Force's main formations were 11th and 36th Brigade Groups of British 78th Division, two regiments of US 34th Division, and No. 1 and No. 6 Commando battalions, recently integrated with American members. Once consolidated ashore, Eastern Task Force became British First Army and would field Crusader III and Valentine tanks as well as Britain's 1st Parachute Brigade. Long fully mobilized, the British Army of 1942 was weary and seasoned, although much experience had been defeat and withdrawal, however skillful. None of the units or commanders assigned to *Torch* had previous North Africa experience; Anderson would employ "task force" tactics long discarded by Eighth Army.

In November 1942, the US Army was wholly inexperienced and undergoing massive mobilization. Organization, doctrine, and tactics for armor, antitank, airborne, commando, amphibious, and interservice operations were being developed almost from scratch. Befitting a rich society, US troops were over-equipped and over-reliant on numerical and material superiority; though highly motivated, they were somewhat inflexible to unexpected situations in combat.

Torch would be the US Army's first amphibious operation of World War II. The US Army had only recently begun serious study into amphibious assaults, initially copying the US Marine Corps' tentative doctrine wholesale, then evolving separately. Unlike the USMC, the Army preferred night landings. In 1942, the US Army's basic building block for an amphibious assault was the Regimental Landing Group (RLG), an infantry regiment task-organized via customized combat and support attachments. Each RLG boasted 5,250 troops and 440 vehicles (including a platoon of five M3/M5 light tanks) and was composed of three Battalion Landing Teams (BLTs). An RLG employed two BLTs for the assault with the third BLT retained as a floating reserve. M3 and M4 medium tanks were too large for 1942 tank

lighters; only M3/M5 light tanks assaulted North African beaches. Center Task Force wielded the US 1st Infantry and 1st Armored Divisions. Its medium tanks were the older M3 Lees; after the fall of Tobruk, Roosevelt had shipped the US 1st Armored Division's 232 assigned M4 Shermans to Britain's Eighth Army as a consolation gift. The US Army, having misread blitzkrieg, fielded excessively tank-heavy armor units woefully short of infantry. Five of six US tank destroyer battalions were equipped with the provisional M3 75mm GMC, a 75mm gun mounted on a half-track. Field artillery was an American strength. The US also employed a battalion of paratroopers from the 509th Parachute Infantry Regiment (PIR).

A Twelfth Air Force P-38 Lightning at a muddy North African airfield, December 5, 1942. Aircraft, personnel, and staff of the Twelfth Air Force had originally been assigned to the Eighth Air Force in the UK and were hurriedly transferred to the Mediterranean. By eviscerating the Eighth's 1942 build-up, *Torch* postponed the climax of the USAAF's carefully scheduled strategic bombing offensive against Germany from 1943 to 1944. (Critical Past)

Staging from the United States, Western Task Force's 3rd Infantry, 9th Infantry, and 2nd Armored Divisions were lavishly equipped, receiving the newest ordnance models wherever possible. Unique to Western Task Force were M4 Sherman medium tanks, new M5 Stuart light tanks, M10 tank destroyers, new model AA guns, high-speed artillery tractors, M7 Priest self-propelled 105mm howitzers, bazookas, and more.

By D+3, AFHQ planned to base 90, 160, and 160 aircraft at Algiers, Oran, and Casablanca respectively. On D+42 the Allies would reach their total planned air strength of 1,698 aircraft of all types.

The RAF's Eastern Air Command would cover Algiers and Tunisia with 454 aircraft, including ten Spitfire and four Hurricane IIC fighter squadrons. Air support was provided by two squadrons of mostly Hurricane IIEs with a few Mustang Mk I/IIs. Bristol Beaufighters were *Torch*'s only night fighters. Bristol Blenheim Vs, Lockheed Hudson IIIs, and Vickers Wellington IIIs supplied RAF bomber capability, while Fleet Air Arm Supermarine Walruses and Swordfish IIs were slated for maritime patrol.

The USAAF's Twelfth Air Force would cover Oran and Morocco as the Western Air Command. Twelfth Air Force planned a total of 1,244 aircraft and 75,000 personnel in 19 groups (71 squadrons), including 400 long-range P-38 Lightnings, 240 P-40 Warhawks, and 228 medium bombers, observation-bombers, and reconnaissance aircraft. Beginning D+2, XII Air Support Command would fly aircraft from Gibraltar to Morocco. Planned D+6 strength was 160 fighters, 13 fighter-observation, and 15 light bombers. Once local French air elements were neutralized, 80 fighters were to transfer from Morocco to Oran.

USAAF fighters were lackluster. The brand-new P-38 Lightning was technically advanced but plagued by teething issues. The P-40 Warhawk's pedestrian performance was mitigated by North Africa's low-altitude combat. Six USAAF squadrons had been re-equipped in England with Britain's superb Spitfire, superior to any US fighter in 1942. *Torch*'s assigned P-39 Airacobras were delayed in England until 1943. USAAF bombers and transports were highly effective. A-20 Havocs, B-25 Mitchells, and B-26 Marauders equipped USAAF light and medium bombardment groups; B-17 Flying Fortresses and B-24 Liberators rounded out heavy bombardment units. C-47 Skytrains provided the Allies' entire troop transport capacity. F-4s and F-5s (converted P-38s) supplied US photo recon.

A restored Curtiss Hawk 75 in French markings, though lacking the vertical yellow tail stripe the Luftwaffe required of the Vichy Armée de l'Air. The Indian head insignia identifies the famous Lafayette Escadrille, first established in 1916 for American volunteers. Ironically, the Lafayette Escadrille (GC II/5) was stationed at Casablanca during *Torch* and found itself fighting the American invaders. (Wikimedia Commons, GFDL)

FRENCH

Vichy forces in North Africa were constrained by the Compiègne treaty. Total French personnel in North Africa came to 120,000. French Morocco was allowed 55,000 troops and Algeria 50,000. Tunisia was initially demilitarized at the insistence of the Italians, but was authorized 15,000 troops after the Vichy proved they would defend their colonies against Britain.

The Marine Nationale was Vichy's strongest and most loyal branch. At Casablanca was the incomplete 15in. battleship *Jean Bart*, light cruiser *Primauguet*, seven destroyers, and eight submarines. Bizerte and Oran hosted destroyers, submarines, and smaller craft. At Dakar in French West Africa were the fully operational 15in. battleship *Richelieu*, three cruisers, and three destroyers. Mostly immobilized at Toulon were three battleships, seven cruisers, 28 destroyers, and 15 submarines. French ports were well defended by coastal artillery carefully situated on bluffs and headlands. French airpower and coast artillery posed a real menace to landings; in 1942 successful amphibious assaults in the face of resistance were still historically rare.

The Vichy French air force was experienced and solidly equipped; by Operation *Torch*, there were about 500 aircraft in North Africa, mostly French-built or pre-Vichy American imports. Primary French fighters were the excellent Dewoitine D.520 and obsolete Curtiss Hawk 75 (P-36). Twin-engine bombers were mostly modern LeO 451s and DB-7s (French-modified A-20s).

The strongest land-based French combat arm in North Africa was artillery, appearing as both well-trained field batteries and as fixed coastal fortifications. Seen here at Paris' Musée de l'Armée is a preserved example of the 1897 75mm field gun employed by the Armée d'Afrique. Though antiquated, the revered *Soixante-Quinze* was plentiful and effective. French field artillery would noticeably frustrate Allied operations ashore until the armistice. (PHGCOM, photographed at the Musee de l'Armee)

French troops in North Africa were an organizational and ethnic hodgepodge of all-European, all-colonial, ethnically mixed, and Foreign Legion units. Officers were European but most units and enlisted men colonial. Infantry, called *tirailleurs* (riflemen), were meagerly equipped, without even submachine guns or grenade launchers, but they possessed adequate machine guns. Historically, the French artillery arm was of high quality. Vichy forces in North Africa were short of heavy guns, but possessed ample numbers of the legendary though ancient "French 75." Total field artillery came to 358 guns. Compiègne denied the French medium tanks, relegating Vichy's North-African armor to 335 armored cars and obsolescent light tanks, such as World War I-vintage Renault FTs and 1930s-era Char D1s and Renault R35s. They were modestly inferior to the US M3/M5 light tanks they would fight. French mechanized units were greatly hampered by severe gasoline and spare parts shortages.

AXIS

On November 8, the Axis possessed essentially no combat units in French North Africa, but air and sea units were capable of interfering from Italian bases. By late October 1942, 574 Italian and 298 German aircraft in Sicily and Sardinia could reach Algeria and Tunisia. Luftwaffe fighters were Bf 109F/Gs and Fw 190s, not yet outclassed in 1942. Air support was provided by obsolescent Ju 87 Stuka dive bombers, still potent beneath German fighter cover. Ju 88 and He 111 medium bombers were effective against shipping as well as land targets. The Regia Aeronautica Italiana fielded the modern Macchi C.202 and serviceable Reggiane Re.2001 fighters. The Savoia-Marchetti SM.84, CANT Z.1007 bis, and Ju 87 Stuka equipped Italian bomber units.

The Regia Marina's six battleships, nine cruisers, and 28 destroyers were formidable on paper but tied to port by political timidity and lack of fuel. Additionally, 35 Italian submarines, 15 U-boats, and several fast patrol boat squadrons were stationed in the Mediterranean.

A total of 65,944 Axis personnel would arrive in Tunisia by December 31, 1942. German strength included 47,121 troops, 329 panzers, 3,190 vehicles, and 362 guns. Indoctrinated with mission-type leadership and tactical aggressiveness, the Germans unsurprisingly proved the campaign's finest ground forces. German army (*Heer*) units were equipped with excellent weapons, such as long-barreled 75mm PzKpfw IVs, 88mm Flak (multi-role) guns, and brand-new MG 42 machine guns and Pzkpfw VI Tigers. Italy's main formation in Tunisia would be XXX Corpo, primarily the 1a Divisione di Fanteria Superga and the 50a Brigata Speciale del generale Imperiali; total personnel by December 31, 1942 came to 18,823. Italian martial incompetence was certainly exaggerated by self-serving German and Allied postwar accounts.

A Luftwaffe Heinkel He 111 bomber is seen here, armed with two LF-5B torpedoes. Though often overlooked by English-language histories, the German and Italian torpedo bomber arms were forces to be reckoned with. Concentrated Axis air and submarine attacks would decimate Allied *Torch* shipping after D-Day. (World War II Database)

ORDERS OF BATTLE, NOVEMBER 8, 1942

ALLIED

EASTERN TASK FORCE (BRITISH) (LIEUTENANT-GENERAL KENNETH ANDERSON)

78th Infantry Division (Major-General Vyvyan Evelegh)
11th Infantry Brigade Group
    2nd/Lancashire Fusiliers
    5th/Northamptonshires
    1st/East Surreys
36th Infantry Brigade Group
    5th/The Buffs
    6th/Royal West Kents
    8th/Argyll and Sutherland Highlanders
No. 1 Commando (Lieutenant-Colonel Thomas Trevor)
No. 6 Commando (Lieutenant-Colonel Iain McAlpine)
34th Infantry Division (US) (Major-General Charles Ryder)
168th Infantry Regiment
39th Infantry Regiment
3rd Battalion, 135th Infantry (US) (*Terminal*) (Lieutenant-Colonel Edwin Swenson)

CENTER TASK FORCE (US) (MAJOR-GENERAL LLOYD FREDENDALL)

1st Infantry Division (Major-General Terry Allen)
16th Infantry Regiment
18th Infantry Regiment
26th Infantry Regiment
1st Ranger Battalion
1st Ranger Battalion (Lieutenant-Colonel William O. Darby)
1st Armored Division (Major-General Orlando Ward)
Combat Command B
    Task Force Green
    Task Force Red
3rd/6th Armored Infantry Regiment, Companies G, H (*Reservist*) (Lieutenant-Colonel George F. Marshall)
Parachute Task Force (*Villain*) (Colonel William Bentley, USAAF)
60th Troop Carrier Group (39 x C-47) (Lieutenant-Colonel Thomas Schofield)
2nd/509th Parachute Infantry Regiment (Lieutenant Colonel Edson Raff, US Army)

WESTERN TASK FORCE (US) (MAJOR-GENERAL GEORGE S. PATTON)

Sub-Task Force Goalpost (Major-General Lucian Truscott)
60th Infantry Regiment, 9th Infantry Division
1st/66th Armor Regiment
Sub-Task Force Brushwood (Major-General Jonathan Anderson)
3rd Infantry Division
    7th Infantry Regiment
    30th Infantry Regiment
    15th Infantry Regiment
1st/67th Armor Regiment
436th Coastal Artillery Battalion
2nd/20th Engineer Regiment
Sub-Task Force Blackstone (Major-General Ernest Harmon)
47th Infantry Regiment, 9th Infantry Division
CCB/2nd Armored Division
    2nd/67th Armor Regiment
    3rd/67th Armor Regiment

FORCE H (ROYAL NAVY) (VICE ADMIRAL SIR NEVILLE SYFRET)

CV *Formidable*
    885 Naval Air Squadron (6 x Seafire IIB)
    888 Naval Air Squadron (12 x Martlet IV)
    893 Naval Air Squadron (12 x Martlet IV)
    820 Naval Air Squadron (12 x Albacore)
CV *Victorious*
    809 Naval Air Squadron (6 x Seafire IIB)
    882 Naval Air Squadron (18 x Martlet IV)
    884 Naval Air Squadron (6 x Seafire IIB)
    817 Naval Air Squadron (8 x Albacore)
    832 Naval Air Squadron (8 x Albacore)
BB *Duke of York*
CC *Renown*
CA *Bermuda*
CL *Argonaut*
CL *Sirius*
DD *Eskimo, Ashanti, Tartar, Meteor, Milne, Martin, Lookout, Quentin, Quality, Quiberon, Pathfinder, Opportune, Penn, Panther, Ithuriel, Isaac Sweers*

EASTERN NAVAL TASK FORCE (ROYAL NAVY) (VICE ADMIRAL HAROLD BURROUGH)

Naval Support Force
CVL *Argus*
    880 Naval Air Squadron (18 x Seafire IIB)
CVE *Avenger*
    802 Naval Air Squadron (6 x Sea Hurricane II)
    883 Naval Air Squadron (8 x Sea Hurricane II)
CL *Sheffield*
CL *Scylla*
CL *Charybdis*
DD *Vanoc, Wrestler, Clare, Enchantress*
DS *Ibis*
DC *Spey, Marigold, Convolvulus, Samphire, Penstemon*
Western Landing Group (Captain N. V. Dickinson)
Apples Sector Landing Support Force
    AAS *Pozarica*
    AMT *Rysa, Juliet, Stroma*
    DC *Rother*
    DE *Bicester, Bramham*
    AM *Cadmus*
    SS *P 221*
Apples Sector Landing Force (11th BG)
    LSI(L) *Karanja, Viceroy of India, Marnix Van Sint Aldegonde* (Dutch)
    LSG *Dewdale*
    Transports *Manchester, Lalande, Ocean Wanderer, Ocean Victory*
Center Landing Group (Captain Robert Shaw)
Beer Sector Naval Landing Support Force
    BM *Roberts*
    AAS *Palomares*
    DD *Błyskawica* (Polish)
    DE *Lamerton, Wheatland, Wilton*
    AM *Acute, Alarm, Albacore, Hoy, Incholm, Mull*
    SS *P 48*
Beer Sector Naval Landing Force (168th RCT)
    LSH *Bulolo*
    LSI(L) *Keren, Winchester Castle, Otranto, Awatea*
    Transports *Strathnever, Sobieski* (Polish), *Cathay, Ennerdale, Sobo, Jean Jadot* (Belgian), *Tiba* (Dutch), *Loch Mona, Urlana, Glenfinlas, Stanhill, City of Worcester, Ocean Volga, Ocean Rider*
Eastern Landing Group (Captain C. D. Edgar, USN)
Charlie Sector Naval Support Force
    AAS *Tynwald*
    DE *Cowdray, Zetland*
    AM *Algerine, Hussar, Speedwell, Cava, Othello*

SS *P 45*
Charlie Sector Naval Landing Force (39th RCT)
    APA *Samuel Chase* (US Coast Guard), *Thomas Stone* (US)
    AP *Leedstown* (US)
    AK *Almaack* (US)
    Transports *Exceller* (US), *Demo* (Dutch), *Macharda, Maron*
Operation *Terminal* (Royal Navy) (3rd/135th Infantry Regiment,
    US 9th Division) (Captain Henry St John Fancourt, RN)
    DD *Broke, Malcolm*

CENTER NAVAL TASK FORCE (ROYAL NAVY) (COMMODORE THOMAS TROUBRIDGE)

Naval Support Force
BB *Rodney*
CV *Furious*
    801 Naval Air Squadron (12 x Seafire IC)
    807 Naval Air Squadron (12 x Seafire IIB)
    822 Naval Air Squadron (8 x Albacore)
CVE *Biter*
    800 Naval Air Squadron (15 x Sea Hurricane II)
CVE *Dasher*
    804 Naval Air Squadron (6 x Sea Hurricane II)
    891 Naval Air Squadron (6 x Sea Hurricane II)
CL *Jamaica*
AAS *Alynbank*
DD *Boreas, Bulldog, Beagle, Boadicea, Amazon, Achates,*
    Antelope, Wescott
DE *Farndale, Calpe, Avon Vale, Puckeridge*

Western Landing Group (Captain G. R. C. Allen)
X Sector Naval Support Force
    CL *Aurora*
    DD *Wivern*
    DC *Gardenia, Vetch*
X Sector Naval Landing Force (Task Force Green)
    LSI(L) *Batory* (Polish), *Princess Beatrix*
    LSI(M) *Queen Emma*
    LST *Bachaquero*
    Transports *Benalbenach, Mary Slessor, Mark Twain* (US),
    Walt Whitman (US)

Center Landing Group (Captain E. V. Lees)
Y Sector Naval Support Force
    DD *Brilliant, Verity*
    AM *Eday, Inchmarinock, Kerrera, Coriolanus*
Y Sector Landing Force (26th RCT)
    LSI(L) *Glengyle, Monarch of Bermuda, Llangibby Castle*
    Transports *Clan MacTaggart, Salacia*

Eastern Landing Group (Captain C. D. Graham)
Z Sector Naval Support Group
    CL *Delhi*
    DD *Vansittart*
    DS *Aberdeen, Deptford*
    DC *Exe, Swale, Rhododendron, Violet*
Z Sector Naval Landing Force (16th RCT, 18th RCT, Task Force Red)
    LSI(H) *Royal Scotsman, Royal Ulsterman, Ulster Monarch*
    LSI(L) *Reina del Pacifico, Ettrick, Durban Castle, Warwick Castle,*
    Duchess of Bedford
    Transport *Tegelberg* (Dutch)
    LSG *Derwentdale*
    LST *Misoa, Tasajera*
Z Sector Slow Convoy
    Transports *Alcinous* (Dutch), *Charles H. Cramp* (US), *Chattanooga*
    City, Delilah, Derbyshire, Edward Rutledge (US), *Empire*
    Confidence, Empire Mordred, Havildar, Letitia, Lycaon, Mootian,
    Nieuw Zeeland (Dutch), *Pacific Explorer, St. Essylt, Theseus, William*
    Floyd (US), *William Wirt* (US), *Zebulon B. Vance* (US)
Operation *Reservist* (3rd/6th Armored Infantry Regiment,
    Companies G, H)
    DS *Walney, Hartland*

WESTERN NAVAL TASK FORCE (USN TASK FORCE 34) (US NAVY) (REAR ADMIRAL HENRY "KENT" HEWITT)

Northern Attack Group (TG 34.8) (Rear Admiral Monroe Kelly)
BB *Texas*
CL *Savannah*
DesRon 11
    DD *Roe, Livermore, Kearny, Ericsson, Parker*
Air Group
    ACV *Sangamon*
    VT-26 (9 x TBF, 9 x SBD)
    ACV *Chenango*
    USAAF 33rd FG (77 x P-40)
    DesDiv 19
    DD *Hambleton, Macomb*
DD *Dallas, Eberle*
Freighter SS *Contessa* (Honduran)
TransDiv 5 (Sub-Task Force Goalpost)
    AP *Henry T. Allen, John Penn, George Clymer, Anthony, Florence*
    Nightingale, Anne Arundel
    AK *Electra, Algorab*
SS *Shad*
AO *Kennebec*
AM *Raven, Osprey*

Covering Group (TG 34.1) (Rear Admiral Robert Giffen)
BB *Massachusetts*
CA *Tuscaloosa*
CA *Wichita*
DesRon 8
    DD *Mayrant, Rhind, Wainwright, Jenkins*
AO *Chemung*

Air Group (TG 34.2) (Rear Admiral Ernest McWhorter)
CV *Ranger*
    VT-41 (1 x TBF, 18 x SBD-3)
    VF-41 (27 x F4F-4)
    VF-9 (27 x F4F-4)
ACV *Suwanee*
    VT-27 (9 x TBF)
    VF-27 (9 x F4F-4)
    VF-28 (9 x F4F-4)
    VF-30 (9 x F4F-4)
CL *Cleveland*
DesDiv 10
    DD *Ellyson, Forrest, Fitch, Corry, Hobson*
SS *Gunnel, Herring*
AO *Winooski*

Center Attack Group (TG 34.9) (Captain Robert Emmet)
CA *Augusta*
CL *Brooklyn*
DesRon 25
    DD *Ludlow, Wilkes, Swanson, Murphy*
DesRon 13
    DD *Rowan, Woolsey, Edison, Bristol, Boyle, Tillman*
Naval Landing Force
    AP *Leonard Wood, Thomas Jefferson*
TransDiv 3 (Sub-Task Force Brushwood)
    AP *William P. Biddle, Joseph T. Dickman, Tasker M. Bliss,*
    Hugh L. Scott, Joseph Hewes, Edward Rutledge, Charles Carroll
TransDiv 9 (Sub-Task Force Brushwood)
    AP *Ancon, Elizabeth C. Stanton, Thurston*
    AK *Arcturus, Procyron, Oberon*
MinRon 7
DMS *Palmer, Hogan, Stansbury*
CM *Miantonomah, Terror*
AM *Auk*

Southern Attack Group (TG 34.10) (Rear Admiral Lyal Davidson)
BB *New York*
CL *Philadelphia*
DesRon 15
    DD *Mervine, Knight, Beatty*
DesDiv 30

DD *Quick, Cowie, Doran, Cole, Bernadou*
Air Group
    ACV *Santee*
    VT-29 (8 x TBF, 9 x SBD)
    VF-29 (14 x F4F-4)
    DD *Rodman, Emmons*
Landing Force (Sub-Task Force Blackstone)
    AP *Harris, Calvert, Dorothea L. Dix, Lyon*
    AK *Titania*
    Seatrain *Lakehurst* (55 x M4 Sherman)
CM *Monadnock*
DMS *Howard, Hamilton*
AO *Housatonic, Merrimack*
SS *Barb*
AT *Cherokee*

FRENCH

ARMÉE DE L'ARMISTICE: ARMÉE D'AFRIQUE (GÉNÉRAL DE CORPS ALPHONSE JUIN)

XIXe Région Militaire (Général de corps Louis-Marie Koeltz)
Division d'Alger (Général de division Charles Mast)
    1er Régiment de Zouaves
    1er Régiment de Tirailleurs Algériens
    5e Régiment de Tirailleurs Algériens
    9e Régiment de Tirailleurs Algériens
    13e Régiment de Tirailleurs Sénégalais
    29e Régiment de Tirailleurs Algériens
    65e Régiment d'Artillerie d'Afrique
    5e Régiment de Chasseurs d'Afrique
    1er Régiment de Spahis Algériens
    III/7e Régiment de la Garde
    II/411e Régiment d'Artillerie d'Afrique
    1er Sapeurs Annamites
Division de Constantine (Général de division Joseph Edouard Welvert)
    15e Régiment de Tirailleurs Sénégalais
    3e Régiment de Tirailleurs Algériens
    3e Régiment de Zouaves
    7e Régiment de Tirailleurs Algériens
    67e Régiment d'Artillerie d'Afrique
    3e Régiment de Chasseurs d'Afrique
    3e Régiment de Spahis Algériens
    6e Régiment de Spahis Algériens
    7e Régiment de la Garde
Division d'Oran (Général de division Robert Boissau)
    2e Régiment de Zouaves
    2e Régiment de Tirailleurs Algériens
    6e Régiment de Tirailleurs Algériens
    16e Régiment de Tirailleurs Algériens
    66e Régiment de Tirailleurs Algériens
    2e Régiment de Spahis Algériens
    2e Régiment de Chasseurs d'Afrique
    9e Régiment de Chasseurs d'Afrique
    411e Régiment d'Artillerie d'Afrique

Commandement des Troupes du Maroc (Général de division Georges Lascroux)
Division de Casablanca (Général de division Émile Béthouart)
    1er Régiment de Tirailleurs Marocains
    6e Régiment de Tirailleurs Marocains
    Régiment d'Infanterie Coloniale du Maroc
    III/6e Régiment de Tirailleurs Sénégalais
    1er Régiment de Chasseurs d'Afrique
    3e Régiment de Spahis Marocains
    I/9e Régiment de la Garde
    Régiment d'Artillerie Coloniale du Maroc
Division de Fez (Général de brigade M. M. Salbert)
    4e Régiment de Tirailleurs Marocains
    5e Régiment de Tirailleurs Marocains

    11e Régiment de Tirailleurs Algériens
    III/3e Régiment Étranger d'Infanterie
    1/6e Régiment de Tirailleurs Sénégalais
    1er Régiment Étranger de Cavalerie
    IV/9e Régiment de la Garde
    63e Régiment d'Artillerie d'Afrique
Division de Marrakech (Général de division Henri Martin)
    2e Régiment de Tirailleurs Marocains
    2e Régiment Étranger d'Infanterie
    II/6e Régiment de Tirailleurs Sénégalais
    4e Régiment de Spahis Marocains
    II/9e Régiment de la Garde
    Régiment d'Artillerie Coloniale du Maroc
Division de Meknès (Général de division André Dody)
    7e Régiment de Tirailleurs Marocains
    8e Régiment de Tirailleurs Marocains
    3e Régiment Étranger d'Infanterie
    3e Régiment de Spahis Marocains
    10e Groupe Autonome de Chasseurs d'Afrique
    III/9e Régiment de la Garde
    64e Régiment d'Artillerie d'Afrique

Division de Tunis (Général de division Georges Barré)
Groupement de Bizerte
    43e Régiment d'Infanterie Coloniale
    III/4e Régiment Mixte de Zouaves et Tirailleurs
    III/8e Régiment de la Garde
    II/62e Régiment d'Artillerie d'Afrique
    Fusiliers-Marins
Groupement de Tunis
    I, II/4e Régiment Mixte de Zouaves et Tirailleurs
    II/4e Régiment de Chasseurs d'Afrique
    I/62e Régiment d'Artillerie d'Afrique
    I/412e Régiment d'Artillerie
Groupement de Sahel
    II/4e Régiment de Tirailleurs Tunisiens
    III/4e Régiment de Tirailleurs Tunisiens
    III/4e Régiment de Chasseurs d'Afrique
    I/4e Régiment de Spahis Tunisiens
    II/412e Régiment d'Artillerie
Groupement du Sud Tunisien
    I/4e Régiment de Tirailleurs Tunisiens
    II 4e Régiment de Spahis Tunisiens
Groupement Réservé No 1 (Tunis)
    III/43e Régiment d'Infanterie Coloniale
    I/4e Régiment de Chasseurs d'Afrique
    VII/4e Régiment de Chasseurs d'Afrique
    II/8e Régiment de la Garde
    III/62e Régiment d'Artillerie d'Afrique
Groupement Réservé No 2 (Kairouan)
    II/4e Régiment de Tirailleurs Tunisiens
    III/4e Régiment de Tirailleurs Tunisiens
    V/8e Régiment de la Garde
    III/62e Régiment d'Artillerie d'Afrique

MARINE NATIONALE: 4E RÉGION MARITIME (VICE-AMIRAL JACQUES MOREAU)
Alger (Vice-Amiral Marcel Leclerc)
9e Division de Sous-Marins
    SS *Caïman, Marsouin*
DE/PB *Ch 3, Engagante, La Boudeuse, Sergent Gouarne*
Escadrille 4BR
    (6 x Potez 63.11)
Oran (Vice-Amiral A. G. Rioult)
DD *Epervier*
7e Division de Torpilleurs
    DD *Tramontane, Typhon, Tornade*
    DS/PB *La Surprise, La Bônoise, L'Ajaccienne, La Toulonnaise, La Sétoise*
12e Division de Sous-Marins
    SS *Argonaute, Diane*

5e Division de Sous-Marins
    SS *Actaéon, Fresnel*
Flotille 4F
    (13 x LeO 451)
5th Flotilla
    (13 x Lat 298)
Maroc (Vice-Amiral François Michelier)
BB *Jean Bart*
2e Escadre Légère (Contre-Amiral Raymond de Lafond)
    CL *Primauguet*
    11e Division de Contre-Torpilleurs
    DD *Milan, Albatros*
    2e Division de Torpilleurs
    DE *Fougueux, Frondeur, L'Alcyon*
    5e Division de Torpilleurs
    DE *Brestois, Boulonnais*
    6e Division de Torpilleurs
    DE *Tempête, Simoun*
6e Escadrille d'Avisos
    DE *Commandant Delage, La Gracieuse, La Grandière*
6e Escadrille de Patrouilleurs
    PT *La Servannaise, L'Algéroise, Chasseur 2*
4e Division de Sous-Marins
    SS *Sidi-Ferruch, Le Tonnant, Le Conquérant*
16e Division de Sous-Marins
    SS *La Sibylle, Amazone, L'Amphitrite, Antiope*
17e Division de Sous-Marins
    SS *La Psyché, Oréade, Orphée, Méduse*
Tunisie (Vice-Amiral Edmond-Louis Derrien)
SS *Circé, Calypso, Turquoise, Saphir, Nautilus, Phoque, Espadon,*
    Dauphin, Requin
12e Division de Torpilleurs
    PT *La Pomone, L'Iphigénie, Bombarde*
3e Escadrille d'Avisos
    DS *Commandant Rivière, La Batailleuse*
Escadrille 1E (3 x Bréguet 521, 3 x LeO H.257 bis)

ARMÉE DE L'AIR: 1ER RÉGION AÉRIENNE (GÉNÉRAL DE DIVISION JEAN MENDIGAL)

Algérie, Groupe Mixte 26
Groupe de Chasse II/3 (22 x Dw.520)
Groupe de Chasse III/6 (25x Dw.520)
Groupe de Bombardement I/19 (13 x DB-7)
Groupe de Bombardement II/61 (13 x DB-7, 2 x LeO 451)
Groupe de Transport II/15 (17 x Potez 540, 3 x Potez 650)
Algérie, Groupe Mixte 3
Groupe de Chasse III/3 (26 x Dw.520)
Groupe de Bombardement I/11 (13 x LeO 451)
Groupe de Reconnaissance II/52 (9 x Bloch 175, 2 x Bloch 174)
Groupe de Reconnaissance I/36 (6 x Po 63.11)
Maroc, Groupe Mixte 11
Groupe de Chasse I/5 (26 x Curtiss H-75)
Groupe de Chasse II/5 (20 x Curtiss H-75, 13 x Dw 520)
Groupe de Bombardement I/23 (13 x LeO 451)
Groupe de Bombardement II/23 (13 x LeO 451)
Groupe de Bombardement I/32 (13 x DB-7)
Groupe de Bombardement II/32 (13 x LeO 451)
Groupe de Reconnaissance I/22 (13 x LeO 451)
Groupe de Reconnaissance I/52 (13 x Po 63.11)
Groupe de Transport I/15 (18 x Po 29, 5 x F222, 1 x F224)
Groupe de Transport III/15 (4 x Amiot 143)
Tunisie, Groupe Mixte 8
Sidi Ahmed: Groupe de Chasse II/7 (26x Dw.520)
Escadrille de Chasse de Nuit 3/13 (8 x Po 631)
Groupe de Bombardement I/25 (13 x LeO 451)
Groupe de Bombardement II/25 (13 x LeO 451)
Groupe de Bombardement II/33 (11 x Bloch 174)

OPPOSING PLANS

ALLIED

The Combined Chiefs' August 13 directive to Eisenhower epitomized the *Torch* mission: "The President and the Prime Minister have agreed that combined military operations be directed against Africa as early as practicable with a view to gaining, in conjunction with Allied forces in the Middle East, complete control of North Africa from the Atlantic to the Red Sea." The *Torch* expedition was to be the beginning of a major new long-term commitment to the Mediterranean theater; Algeria and Morocco would become staging areas for future Allied operations.

The Allies expected to descend on French North Africa suddenly and with overwhelming force, not just ensuring military victory but shocking the French into accepting a political fait accompli. Within a few days, the Allies would concentrate as many troops ashore as were dispersed garrisoning all of French North Africa. Still, *Torch* was operating on a shoestring; referring to global commitments, Churchill remarked to Roosevelt, "You too have cut yourself to the bone."

Eastern, Center, and Western Task Forces would initially be supported by naval gunfire and naval air support until replaced by land-based RAF and USAAF air support transferred to captured airfields. One must note the Allies

RIGHT
Two iconic American weapons: a jeep rolls off a Higgins LCVP at Fedala, probably November 8, 1942. Note the jeep's fitted snorkel allowing it to ford shallow water. Of the Higgins boat, Eisenhower later remarked the war could not have been won without them. Over 20,000 would be built. (LOC)

FAR RIGHT
In July 1942, the RAF established the Special Erection Party at Gibraltar for Operation *Torch*. On October 28, the first shipment of 116 Spitfires and 13 Hawker Hurricanes arrived to be assembled and tested, including these Spitfire Mark Vs. With the help of the Malta Brigade, all aircraft were ready by D-Day, November 8. (IWM CM 6699)

were far from the US Navy's late-war Pacific form, when crushing and highly choreographed air-sea bombardments would methodically batter hostile shores into submission.

Ideally Algiers would be seized quickly without need of Eastern Task Force's floating reserves, which would then leapfrog east towards Tunisian ports as rapidly as possible. The Allies anticipated a swift and urgent Axis reaction that they would need to sweep aside before *Torch*'s offensive stalled. In case Spain moved on the Straits, two British divisions of a special Northern Task Force under Lieutenant-General Frederick Morgan would sortie from England against Spanish Morocco as Operation *Backbone*.

The Gleaves-class destroyer USS *Hambleton* (DD-455) and auxiliary aircraft carrier USS *Sangamon* (ACV-26) en route to Morocco, November 1942. *Torch*'s four US auxiliary carriers were of the Sangamon class, displacing 23,875 tons and carrying about 30 aircraft. They were the first US auxiliary (escort) carriers to see combat. (Navsource)

The Allies hoped to coordinate with local anti-Vichy resistance and a thin in-country network of US State Department personnel. Chief was US consul in Algiers Robert Murphy, who announced American political positions to the French in negotiations prior to the landings:

1. France would be fully restored to her pre-war boundaries and sovereign independence.
2. Purely French national matters would be left for determination by the French without American interference.
3. The "government of the United States regards the French nation as an ally and will deal with it as such."

In French North Africa, Christians, Jews, and Muslims lived side-by-side, as did Europeans and indigenous Arabs and Berbers. Simmering ethno-religious tensions had historically been kept in check by French authority. French administrative control maintained modern civilization in urban areas. Without the experienced local bureaucracies, the Allies knew they could trigger a state of regional anarchy derailing their campaign and undermining their moral cause. The Allies deemed local cooperation essential to keeping civilized control over the region and took pains to educate their troops on how to treat the natives. An American circular announced, "The local population will respect strong, quiet men who live up to their promises. Do not boast nor brag, and keep any agreement you make."

FRENCH

Many accounts of Operation *Torch* trot out a shopworn cliché: that the French fought the Allies for just long enough to sufficiently "satisfy military honor" and then, after meeting some magical benchmark, surrendered to the Allies, chivalry intact – thus implying an actual plan to needlessly extinguish a certain number of lives to no political end. The entire notion is nonsense. Some French commanders and units chose not to fight the Allies; they welcomed the foreign army that might eventually destroy Nazi Germany. Most French units, however, resisted the Allies stubbornly. As faithful soldiers those that fought expected to defend against any invaders as

Partly operational French battleship *Jean Bart* was the US Navy's most conspicuous target on D-Day. Far more dangerous were Casablanca's torpedo-armed nine destroyers and 11 submarines. Only weeks earlier a single Japanese submarine off Guadalcanal had sunk aircraft carrier *Wasp* and crippled battleship *North Carolina*. A similar feat off Casablanca would have imperiled the Moroccan landings. (World War II Database)

long as possible. Typically these units ceased hostilities only when militarily defeated or when a clearly superior French official ordered them to lay down their arms.

The Vichy government and military took its Compiègne terms of armed neutrality seriously. By November 1942, the Vichy French had resisted British attacks at Mers-el-Kébir, Dakar (September 1940), Syria (June 1941), and Madagascar (May 1942). However, the French military in North Africa was only a garrison force, with no pretensions of waging an offensive campaign.

The aristocratic French navy – undefeated in 1940 – was Vichy's most loyal service. In reality, loyalties of individual military units were determined by their commanders. Some were strongly but secretly pro-Allied. A few were diehards toeing the pro-Axis line out of Vichy. Most were pragmatists and opportunists who, if war came, preferred to await events before they stuck their necks out. Acting on the wrong winner too early invited inevitable treason charges and execution. French officers were career professionals who had served France loyally their entire lives and made personal oaths to Pétain. Consciously deciding to disobey orders from their current government demanded enormous moral courage.

Of North Africa's Frenchmen who desired to fight Vichy and the Axis, there was no centralized group or leader, although the Allies tried to create one in Giraud. Charles de Gaulle's Free France (*France Libre*) was purposely kept unaware of *Torch*, a fact that later angered the general. The US government greatly distrusted de Gaulle; Roosevelt and Leahy referred to him as an "apprentice dictator." French hostile to the Vichy regime were eager to be seen as playing an equal or greater part in liberating their country, best reflected by Giraud's remark, "We don't want the Americans to free us; we want them to help us free ourselves, which is not quite the same." French resistance cells in North Africa were scattered but strongest in Algiers. Members were disproportionately Jewish and Communist and were motivated less by French patriotism than by hatred of Vichy and Nazi policies.

AXIS

France had occupied Tunisia in 1881 over Italian protests. Italian expansionists had long been interested in Tunisia, which they considered a "natural" Italian colony. On the eve of *Torch* two Italian divisions were being held in western Tripolitania in the event an occupation of Tunisia was authorized. Comando Supremo was more concerned with Tunisia's strategic and logistic advantages than with the consequences of antagonizing Vichy; their operational concerns were summarized as "*Malta e nafta*" (Malta and fuel). Italian desire for decisive action in the Mediterranean was restrained by Germany, which preferred a neutral France to any advantages Tunisia might provide in the theater.

Throughout 1942, German focus was on the enormous campaign against the Soviet Union. The Western Desert campaign was a tar-baby born in 1941 as Hitler sought to rescue Mussolini from disaster. Despite Rommel's success, Hitler viewed North Africa as a sideshow, never giving Rommel the resources he needed to decisively defeat Eighth Army. By August 1942, the logistic advantage in North Africa shifted permanently to Britain, precipitating the second battle of El Alamein. In early November, Rommel predicted, "The gradual annihilation of this Army must be expected."

In August 1942, Kriegsmarine chief Erich Raeder warned Hitler of a possible Allied descent on French North Africa. Nevertheless, neither the Wehrmacht nor the Comando Supremo expected the Allies to land there. The Axis grossly underestimated Allied willingness to violate French neutrality and were additionally hoodwinked by the Allies' superior intelligence and elaborate deception campaign. Even as *Torch* convoys traversed the Straits of Gibraltar, their destinations were guessed as Malta, Sicily, Sardinia, or even southern France. Only in the final hours did Comando Supremo alone deduce the massive North Africa invasion. The Wehrmacht possessed no French North Africa contingency plan but had recently formulated *Case Anton*, a plan to occupy all metropolitan France. *Case Anton* derived from updating and combining 1940's Operation *Attila* with Comando Supremo's plan to occupy Corsica, Operation *Camellia*. *Case Anton* was a worst-case scenario; Hitler greatly preferred a warmly neutral France to yet another occupation responsibility.

Benito Mussolini inspects German troops in Sicily, June 1942. The Axis had developed elaborate preparations for Operation *Herkules*, a July 1942 invasion of Malta, and deemed so important by Rommel he had requested to personally lead it. But after Rommel captured Tobruk on June 21, Hitler approved the ill-fated drive into Egypt and *Herkules* was abandoned. (Bundesarchiv, Bild 146-2006-0102 / CC-BY-SA 3.0)

THE CAMPAIGN

The rugged Atlas Mountains extend over a thousand miles from southwest Morocco to Tunisia, cresting at 13,611ft and dividing the mild, semi-arid climate of the Mediterranean coast from the inhospitable Sahara Desert. Shrubby grassland dominates much of the coastal terrain, punctuated by djebels (mountains/hills), wadis (ephemeral river valleys), and sebkhas (endorheic salt flats). In 1942, French North Africa's population was 16.7 million, of whom 15.2 million were Arabs or Berbers, and 1.5 million Europeans and native Jews. About 1 million were French nationals.

An 1827 dispute between the Algerian dey and French consul had escalated into the 1830 French invasion of Algiers, breaking Berber and Ottoman power in western North Africa. The French had never left, eventually expanding into their current North African realm by 1912. Algeria was the jewel of the French empire. As North Africa's most European province, Algeria's Mediterranean coast was an integral part of France, sending three delegates to Paris before the war. Of Algeria's 7.5 million inhabitants, almost 800,000 were French nationals. With a population over 300,000, seedy and sophisticated Algiers was French North Africa's greatest city, the seat of French colonial power, a "reclining woman, white and naked, leaning on her elbow." Algiers' location, European influence, and existing infrastructure made it AFHQ's obvious choice as future headquarters. As the most easterly D-Day objective, Algiers was critical to a decisive advance on Tunisia.

Task Force 34 was the largest war fleet yet dispatched by the United States. Assembled across the East Coast, the ships departed at separate times and took indirect routes; from Bermuda Rear Admiral McWhorter's Air Group resembled "the track of a reeling drunk in the snow." Upon rendezvous 450 miles off Cape Race, the combined armada stretched 30 miles. (US Navy)

FRENCH NORTH AFRICA, D-1

Naval tradition demands admirals give their men a stirring pre-battle speech. On the afternoon of November 7, Western Task Force's Rear Admiral Robert Giffen (US) delivered his:

> The time has now come to prove ourselves worthy of the trust placed in us by our Nation. If circumstances force us to fire upon the French, once our victorious ally, let it be done with the firm conviction that we are striking not at the French people, but at the men who prefer Hitler's slavery to freedom. If we fight, hit hard and break clean. There is glory enough for us all. Good luck. Go with God.

A US Navy chief paraphrased the sentiment for his teenaged gunners: "Come on boys, let's pretend they're Japs!"

To deceive Axis intelligence, Eastern and Center Task Forces steamed past their intended destinations as if headed for Malta, then as night fell on November 7, reversed course to their true objectives. Conflicting intelligence paralyzed Axis decision-making. Despite 76 planes airborne that day and nine U-boats and 26 Italian submarines stationed to intercept, Axis interdiction of the convoys accomplished little. Earlier that morning, a single Luftwaffe He 111 torpedoed the American transport *Thomas Stone*. Eastern Task Force had continued on, Axis bombers hitting but not sinking destroyer HMS *Panther* later that evening. Immobilized 150 miles northwest of Algiers, *Thomas Stone* awaited a tug from Gibraltar, her only escort the corvette HMS *Spey*. *Thomas Stone*'s embarked unit, the US 2nd Battalion, 39th Infantry Regiment, was highly trained and slated for the initial assault.

Aghast at missing D-Day, battalion commander Major Walter Oakes decided to make the remaining 150 miles to Algiers in the 24 landing craft, just in time for the morning assault. Oakes and his 700 men embarked at dusk. Led by *Spey*, the makeshift flotilla set off through the night toward Algiers. Engines broke down while navigation and discipline failed in the dark. By dawn November 8, with surf rising and his men seasick and disorganized, Oakes conceded defeat. *Spey* took the battalion aboard and continued towards Algiers, towing two landing craft and scuttling the rest. Oakes' men missed D-Day but participated in subsequent *Torch* operations. Admiral Cunningham later admitted Oakes' attempt was a "notably courageous decision." Royal Navy destroyers *Velox* and *Wishart* arrived to assist *Thomas Stone* two hours after the landing craft departed. All would arrive safely off Algiers by November 11.

The evening of November 7, a complex anti-Vichy revolt simmered throughout French North Africa. From illegal radios, Resistance members heard the BBC's French voice repeatedly announce, "*Allô Robert* – Franklin arrive." Broadcasting from battleship *Texas*, Allied radio blared, "*Allô, Maroc!*" and looped *La Marseillaise* and *The Star-Spangled Banner*. At 0120hrs, a French voice claiming to be Eisenhower announced that the Americans had arrived to liberate their country, horrifying assault troops across three task forces who concluded surprise was destroyed. A French-speaking Roosevelt exhorted, "*Mes amis* ... have faith in our words. Help us where you are able ... all men who hate tyranny ... join with the liberators who at this moment are about to land on your shores ... *Vive la France éternelle!*"

A view of Algiers' waterfront, c.1942. The US Navy and Royal Navy already shared similar victorious histories here, winning separate wars against the notorious Christian-enslaving Barbary pirates in 1815 and 1816 respectively. (DA Bell, DSM, RNVR courtesy www.captainwalker.uk)

For a year, the inexhaustible Robert Murphy had riskily and tirelessly recruited anti-Vichy officers, politicians, and civilians throughout French North Africa. In the Moroccan capital Rabat, pro-Allied conspirator Général de division Émile Béthouart arrested his superior, Général de division Georges Lascroux, at 0100hrs, November 8. Béthouart's next target was Général de division Louis Lahouelle, Morocco's Armée de l'Air commander. Indecisive about supporting the Americans, Lahouelle telephoned Vice-Amiral François Michelier in Casablanca. Angered, Michelier refused to cooperate and hung up. Lahouelle then refused and Béthouart arrested him also. Back in Casablanca, an alarmed Michelier ordered maximum readiness and to resist any invaders.

At 0230hrs, French Resident-General of Morocco Charles Noguès opened a letter from Béthouart announcing that the Americans were coming, Giraud would take French command against the Axis, and Béthouart had been named Moroccan commander. Overlooked on his desk was an unopened letter from Roosevelt informing Noguès of the Allies' imminent arrival and urging his defection. Noguès confirmed via telephone his Meknès and Marrakech generals remained loyal and assessed Béthouart had been duped. Noguès ordered a general alert. When Béthouart arrived in person to persuade him, Noguès had Béthouart arrested.

In Port Lyautey, Morocco at 0130hrs, Béthouart had ordered 1er RTM commander Colonel Jean Petit to support the American landings. As Petit later recalled, "My surprise, I admit, was total. My emotion considerable." Petit described local authorities as reacting with "an explosion of general joy." But by 0430hrs, Petit was informed that Vice-Amiral Michelier had countermanded Béthouart and ordered Morocco to resist the landings. Stunned and devastated, Petit ordered his troops to fight the Americans, "regardless of how hard and cruel it was." Petit's emotional ordeal would be played out many times throughout French North Africa that morning.

At midnight in Algiers, 20-year-old medical student José Aboulker produced fraudulent paperwork authorizing his Resistance members to seize government buildings. Murphy had promised the group 20 tons in small arms and walkie-talkies via a British submarine. These never arrived; nor did that night's expected 2,000 insurgents. But Aboulker "had dreamed of that night, as one dreams of glory when one is twenty." The 377 members present dispersed through Algiers in buses. Sixteen hijacked the central telephone exchange, another group claimed the governor general's headquarters at the Palais d'Été (Summer Palace), and Aboulker's band seized the main police station. The rebels also arrested Algeria's military commander-in-chief, Général de corps Louis-Marie Koeltz. By 0300hrs, the Resistance had temporarily paralyzed Algiers' command and communications. Their survival depended on the Allies arriving within hours.

Outside Algiers, local anti-Vichy officer candidates had arrested Général de corps Alphonse Juin at his Lambiridi home. Murphy arrived at 0030hrs and announced that a huge American invasion fleet would appear within the hour by express invitation of Général Giraud. Juin was inclined to support the Allies, but wished to consult Vichy commander-in-chief Jean-François

Darlan. Coincidentally, Darlan was in Algiers, visiting his son who was deathly ill with polio. Juin telephoned Darlan, who appeared at Juin's. Initially shocked and angered, Darlan agreed to cooperate with the Allies if Pétain agreed. As Juin, Murphy, and Darlan negotiated, Vichy police arrived and arrested Murphy and the officer candidates. Darlan reported the situation to Pétain in France, who received Roosevelt's envoy announcing the United States' friendly intentions at 0900hrs that morning. Pétain replied that the French empire would resist any invaders and severed relations with the United States.

EASTERN TASK FORCE

Algiers was protected by 13 fortified coastal batteries, the most formidable at Cap Sidi Ferruch, Fort Duperré, and Cap Matifou. Within Algiers were 7,000 French troops, as well as light tanks and armored cars. Outside the city were another 8,000 troops. Nearby Maison Blanche and Blida airfields hosted 47 D.520 fighters and 34 bombers.

British planners had inserted two audacious nighttime coups de main to pre-emptively seize the docks at Algiers and Oran. At Algiers, destroyer *Broke* would ram the boom protecting the harbor, penetrate to the southern basin, and unload US troops at the Quai de Dieppe. Fifteen minutes later, destroyer *Malcolm* would steer for the Grand Môle. The Americans would establish a perimeter, then secure various facilities along the waterfront. The Algiers mission was given the unfortunate codename Operation *Terminal* and ominously scheduled three hours after Eastern Task Force's amphibious landings. Algiers' harbor was ringed by coastal artillery perfectly situated on the city's high bluffs. The Allies hoped the beach landings would draw defenders from the port, while the coastal batteries were expected to be neutralized by commandos before the destroyers arrived.

Operation Terminal, November 8
Late on the afternoon of November 7, the *Terminal* assault teams transferred from cruiser HMS *Sheffield* to the British destroyers *Broke* and *Malcolm*. Lieutenant-Colonel Edwin Swenson (US) commanded an assault force of 662 Americans of the 3rd Battalion, 135th Infantry Regiment, three British Army officers, and 74 Royal Navy personnel. Captain Henry Fancourt (RN) commanded the entire force.

Broke and *Malcolm* started towards Algiers at 0140hrs, November 8. Suddenly, Algiers' lights vanished. Searchlights found the two destroyers and French coastal artillery opened fire. Blinded and deafened by the nighttime bedlam of firepower, the vessels twice missed the harbor entrance. Circling a third time, *Malcolm* was hit hard at 0400hrs and set ablaze. She withdrew with ten dead and 25 wounded. Now alone, *Broke* found the entrance on her fourth attempt and tore through the boom at full speed. Racing into Algiers harbor, she berthed along the Môle Louis Billiard. *Broke*'s assault team landed at 0530hrs and dispersed, seizing the mole, electric power station, and tank farm before extending their perimeter, despite French small arms fire.

HMS *Malcolm* en route to Algiers on the afternoon of November 7, 1942 to execute Operation *Terminal*. The Royal Navy destroyer has just taken aboard more than 300 Americans of the US 3rd Battalion, 135th Infantry Regiment from HMS *Sheffield*. The Allies' repeated difficulties in seizing port facilities intact eventually convinced *Overlord* planners to develop ingenious over-the-beach logistics measures, such as PLUTO and Mulberry. (IWM A 012881)

Eastern Task Force landings at Algiers, November 8, 1942.

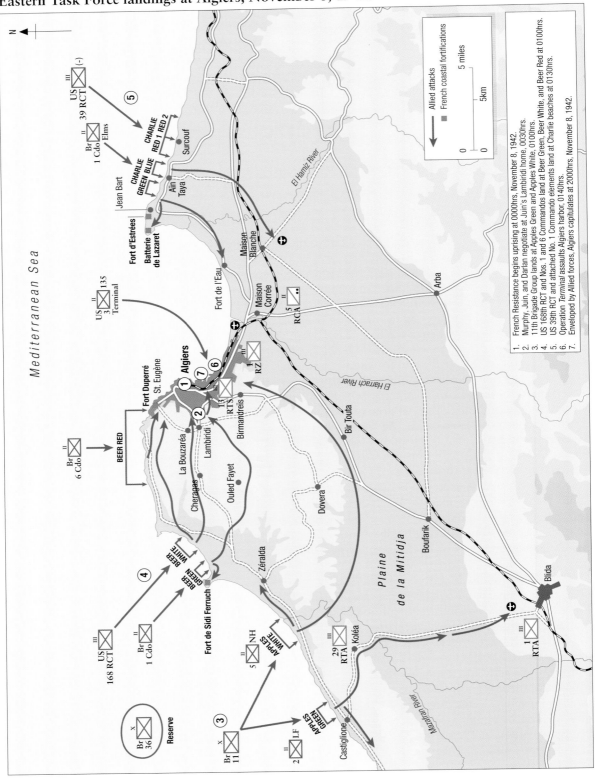

1. French Resistance begins uprising at 0000hrs, November 8, 1942.
2. Murphy, Juin, and Darlan negotiate at Juin's Lambiridi home, 0030hrs.
3. 11th Brigade Group lands at Apples Green and Apples White, 0100hrs.
4. US 168th RCT and Nos. 1 and 6 Commandos land at Beer Green, Beer White, and Beer Red at 0100hrs.
5. US 39th RCT and attached No. 1 Commando elements land at Charlie beaches at 0130hrs.
6. Operation *Terminal* assaults Algiers harbor, 0140hrs.
7. Enveloped by Allied forces, Algiers capitulates at 2000hrs, November 8, 1942.

Terminal appeared to have succeeded. But at 0800hrs, French artillery fire erupted, twice driving *Broke* to better-protected moorings before finally hitting her several times. *Broke*'s siren wailed, urging the troops to re-embark. Sixty returned before *Broke* fled to open sea at 0920hrs. Six Albacore dive bombers covered *Broke*'s withdrawal by knocking out the harbor's northern guns at 1100hrs. Surrounded by Senegalese infantry and low on ammunition, Swenson and most troops remained, hoping to be rescued by the 168th RCT. At 1130hrs, French light tanks and armored cars arrived. Swenson surrendered at 1230hrs, but ecstatic French defenders forgot to sabotage the harbor. *Terminal*'s British casualties came to nine dead and 22 wounded; American casualties were 15 dead and 33 wounded. *Broke*, badly damaged, foundered in rough seas the next day.

Landings and occupation of Algiers, November 8

The Eastern Task Force approaching Algiers under Vice Admiral Burrough (RN) comprised 33 transports, 32,810 troops (22,950 British), 4,115 vehicles, and 27,291 tons of supplies. Its majority-American assault force under Major-General Ryder (US) would come ashore at three designated landing zones: Apples and Beer sectors west of Algiers, and Charlie sector to the east.

Farthest west, 7,230 troops of the British 11th Brigade Group departed transports *Karanja*, *Viceroy of India*, and *Marnix van Suit Aldegonde*. The 2nd Battalion, Lancashire Fusiliers, and 5th Battalion, Northamptonshire Regiment landed at beaches Apples Green and Apples White respectively at 0100hrs, November 8. The 2nd/Lancashire Fusiliers were to march 12 miles inland to capture Blida airfield, while the 5th/Northamptonshires' objective was Algiers 25 miles east. Remaining offshore was the 36th Brigade Group, expected to land in Bougie on D+1 provided the Algiers landings went well. The 11th Brigade Group therefore would be the only large British Army formation to participate in the initial *Torch* landings. Before sunrise, 11th Brigade Group units seized Castiglione, Koléa, and Zéralda, as well as bridges, a radio station, and a French barracks, all without resistance.

Colonel John W. O'Daniel's integrated 168th RCT of 4,355 Americans and 1,035 British began landing at 0100hrs at Beer White. Attached to the 168th RCT was part of No. 1 Commando and all of No. 6 Commando, comprising British and Americans. No. 1 Commando came ashore on 168th RCT's left flank, immediately east of Cap Sidi Ferruch. Northwest of Algiers, No. 6 Commando landed at Pointe Pescade, designated Beer Red. Rough seas and landing craft breakdowns delayed their advance. They reached their objective of Fort Duperré only at 0815hrs, and would not capture it until softened up that afternoon by eight Royal Navy Albacores. By then, 1st Battalion, 168th RCT had reached Lambiridi, before being pinned down all day by spirited French resistance. The 1st/168th RCT's commander, Lieutenant-Colonel Edward Doyle, led a 25-man detachment around Lambiridi and into Algiers, capturing the Palais d'Été at 1500hrs. As Doyle pressed on towards the German consul at the police station, a French sniper shot and killed him.

East of Algiers, nervous and inexperienced Americans of the US 39th RCT hit dry land at Surcouf, November 8, 1942. Note the color bearer climbing the sand berm. Twenty-eight months later, this same regiment would cross the Rhine. (World War II Today)

Meanwhile, pro-Allied French general Charles Mast ordered his troops to stand down and personally greeted Colonel O'Daniel's 168th RCT on the beaches, instructing them where to go and commandeering local transport to facilitate 11th Brigade Group's inland movement. Mast convinced Lieutenant-Colonel Thomas Trevor, No. 1 Commando, to execute an unplanned mission to take Blida airdrome with Mast's requisitioned French vehicles. Trevor's group reached Blida at 0900hrs. Blida's pro-Allied commander Colonel Montrelet had received orders from Mast at 0300hrs to hand over his airfield to the Allies, before receiving a second phone call ordering him to resist. A freed Koeltz had relieved Mast and replaced him with Général Roubertie; the Division d'Alger was now ordered to resist the Allies vigorously. Indecisive, Montrelet allowed Allied aircraft to land but not operate.

Colonel Benjamin F. Caffey, Jr's 39th RCT was to envelop Algiers from the east. Under Caffey's command were 5,668 troops, plus 198 British and 114 Americans of the integrated No. 1 Commando. *Thomas Stone*'s disabling left Caffey short one battalion and his best-trained transport. Disembarking from transports *Samuel Chase*, *Leedstown*, *Almaack*, and *Exceller*, the assault waves landed at Charlie sector east of Cap Matifou at 0130hrs. The transports closed to within 4,000 yards of the beaches when French searchlights and artillery opened up. Trading fire, British destroyers *Cowdray* and *Zetland* knocked out the searchlight and silenced Batterie du Lazaret.

Caffey's No. 1 Commando attachments secured the town of Jean-Bart and the approaches to Fort d'Estrées and Batterie du Lazaret, but were unable to compel their surrender. Meanwhile 3rd Battalion, 39th RCT progressed six miles to Fort de l'Eau before being stopped by French infantry and three tanks. The 1st Battalion, 39th RCT, minus heavy equipment stranded on the beaches, marched ten miles inland to the Maison Blanche airfield by 0615hrs. Several French tanks resisted half-heartedly, then withdrew. The airfield was secured at 0830hrs. Eighteen Hurricanes of RAF No. 43 Squadron arrived at 1035hrs and began air patrols that evening, but the Royal Navy continued to provide most D-Day fighter cover.

With No. 1 Commando's detachments stymied by Fort d'Estrées and Batterie du Lazaret, destroyer *Zetland* commenced an hour-long bombardment at 1030hrs. *Formidable*'s Albacores and cruiser *Bermuda* followed at 1430hrs. Within a few hours, No. 1 Commando captured Batterie du Lazaret and 50 French marines but failed to take the fort by nightfall. The Luftwaffe struck at dusk when 50 Ju 88s, six He 111s, and 14 Italian S.79 torpedo bombers mounted a large-scale attack on Allied shipping offshore. The Axis lost six aircraft but successfully bombed destroyer *Cowdray* and torpedoed transport *Leedstown*, killing eight and wounding 14.

Major-General Ryder had gone ashore from *Bulolo* at 0900hrs. By evening, 5th/Northamptonshires and part of 1st Battalion, East Surreys had reached Algiers' outskirts. Despite setbacks, Allied success was imminent. Authorized by Darlan, Juin wished to negotiate that evening. The Americans took control of Algiers under lenient terms at 2000hrs, relying on French civil assistance and the faith of the French military to abide the truce. Darlan stressed the ceasefire only held for Algiers but agreed to receive the Eastern Task Force in port at dawn.

CENTER TASK FORCE

Oran, population 200,000, had been under French rule since 1831. Algeria's second-largest city was situated in a broad bay, backed by steep bluffs and rugged mountains. Southwest of Oran lay the Sebkha d'Oran, a muddy, 25-mile-long salt lake basin.

Attacking Oran was the Allies' Center Task Force of 44 transports, 40,800 troops (3,740 British), 2,843 vehicles, and 12,601 tons of supplies. French defenses included the 16,700-strong Division d'Oran, 45 fortified coastal guns at Oran, six guns 20 miles east at Arzew, and about 100 planes at the La Sénia, Tafaraoui, and Arzew airbases.

Operation Reservist, November 8

Center Task Force's nighttime harbor sneak attack was Operation *Reservist*. Unlike *Terminal*, *Reservist*'s raiding vessels, the Royal Navy's *Walney* and *Hartland*, were unarmored sloops, not destroyers. More ominously, while Algiers' port faced a large, broad bay, Oran's was a constricted, four-mile-long artificial harbor.

No operational aspect of *Torch* was as controversial as *Reservist*. The US Navy opposed the mission. US Rear Admiral Andrew Bennett, slated to command Oran after capture, vigorously protested *Reservist* as "suicidal and absolutely unsound," disparaging the mission as "The Charge of the 700;" he was supported by Admiral Harold Stark. A third US admiral protested to Eisenhower, who replied, "I can't take your advice on this thing, I have to get my advice from Ramsay." *Torch* deputy naval chief Vice Admiral Bertram Ramsay mused, "If it doesn't do anything else, it's good for the spirit of the people to carry out one of these operations. If successful, it's a wonderful boost for morale." Clark strongly supported *Reservist*, adding that if the French fired on the sloops, they were to withdraw. *Reservist*'s troops were drawn from Major-General Orlando Ward's US 1st Armored Division; Ward, too, protested until admonished by Clark, finally conceding, "My conscience is clear on this matter." The Royal Navy tried to soften *Reservist* by referring to it as "more a Trojan horse operation than an assault." Morison claimed the British considered *Reservist* a commando-type raid but forgot commandos hit and run, while *Reservist* would penetrate Oran to stay.

Commanding *Reservist* was its main planner, Captain Frederic Peters (RN). Clark's assertion aside, the vainglorious Peters had no intentions of retiring in the event of resistance; in addition to accomplishing his charged missions, Peters planned to personally accept the city of Oran's surrender. *Reservist*'s main assault force was 393 Americans of 3rd Battalion, 6th Armored Infantry Regiment, commanded by Lieutenant-Colonel George F. Marshall (no relation to the US Army Chief of Staff). Additional assault team members were four US Navy officers and 22 seamen, six US Marines, and 52 Royal Navy officers and ratings. *Reservist* was scheduled for 0245hrs, November 8, two hours after the initial

HMS *Formidable*'s Martlets and Seafires prepare for launch off the coast of Algeria, November 1942. Mediocre prewar administration forced the Fleet Air Arm to adopt the US Navy's Wildcat (Martlet) and adapt land-based fighters with poor carrier-handling characteristics, such as the Spitfire. (IWM TR 285)

Commissioned into the Royal Navy on May 12, 1941, the unarmored sloop HMS *Walney* is seen here prior to *Torch*. Her light armament of one 5in. gun, one 3in. gun, and two 6-pdrs was sufficient for her originally assigned Sierra Leone–UK convoy route, but grossly inadequate for the *Reservist* mission. (Wikimedia Commons)

HMS *WALNEY*, OPERATION *RESERVIST*, NOVEMBER 8, 1942 (PP. 38–39)

Convinced Oran's port could be captured in one fell swoop before the French sabotaged it, British planners concocted Operation *Reservist*. In the early dark of D-Day, Royal Navy sloops *Walney* and *Hartland* would sneak US infantry into the harbor, seizing Oran's port facilities before the French knew what was happening. The plan's success hung on complete surprise.

HMS *Walney* (**1**) and HMS *Hartland* (**2**) pushed into Oran's port at 0245hrs, November 8, 1942. *Walney* sought the dark cover of the portside cliffs. French machine-gun fire opened up. Lieutenant Paul Duncan (RN) announced through *Walney*'s loudspeaker, "*Ne tirez pas. Nous sommes vos amis. Nous sommes les Américains.*" At 0300hrs, *Walney*'s skipper Lieutenant-Commander Peter Meyrick ordered, "Lie flat for crash; we are approaching the boom." *Walney* sliced through both harbor booms; moments later French fire killed Duncan.

Walney pushed through the harbor's searchlight beams and persisting machine-gun fire. *Walney* was almost to the Môle Central, where her target awaited to port, the moored destroyer *Épervier*. Tied-up French destroyers, submarines, and patrol craft surrounded the darkened *Walney* in a potential three-sided point-blank firing sack. *Walney* readied to drop boats of 14 men each to board and neutralize *Épervier*, while 16 US infantry, including

Lieutenant-Colonel Marshall, hid behind an improvised wall of sandbags at *Walney*'s bow, prepared to lob grenades at *Épervier* in support of the boarding party.

Suddenly, *Épervier*'s probing searchlight found *Walney*'s American flag. *Walney* raked *Épervier*'s deck with a machine gun, then laced *Épervier*'s bridge. *Épervier* and the numerous French warships moored nearby inevitably retaliated with an avalanche of point-blank, multi-caliber shellfire from port, starboard, and ahead, illustrated here. One of *Walney*'s davit-suspended boarding boats was quickly shot into the water, taking its occupants with it. *Walney* succeeded in setting *Tramontane*'s stern afire, but French shells wrecked *Walney*'s bridge and exploded in the sloop's engine room, leaving *Walney* powerless. Remorseless French fire shredded *Walney*'s superstructure, slaughtering US infantry topside and cutting down emerging crew desperate to escape the inferno below. Survivors plunged into the water. Among them was *Reservist*'s commander Captain Frederic Peters, *Walney*'s only bridge survivor. Ablaze from stem to stern, *Walney* drifted lifelessly across the harbor before sinking. *Walney* had absorbed almost 60 point-blank hits from 138mm, 130mm, and 100mm naval guns as well as being struck by some 3,000 machine-gun and small-arms rounds. *Reservist* had been an Allied disaster.

American landings. The French would likely be alerted but not yet aware of the enormous odds they faced. Admiral Cunningham later conceded, "The moment chosen could hardly have been less fortunate."

Defiantly flying both the Stars and Stripes and the White Ensign, Peters' flagship *Walney* opened the port charge just before 0300hrs, *Hartland* behind her. Missing the 200-yard-wide harbor entrance, the sloops circled for a second attempt when Peters received the unhelpful message from Commodore Troubridge, "No shooting thus far; landings unopposed. Don't start a fight unless you have to."

The consequences of wishful thinking: the sunken HMS *Walney* lies capsized in Oran Harbor, November 22, 1942. *Walney* and her sister *Hartland* were two of ten Lake-class US Coast Guard cutters loaned to Britain in 1941, where they were redesignated Banff-class sloops. As USCGC *Sebago*, *Walney* had once trained cadets at the United States Coast Guard Academy in New York. (IWM A 013693)

Half a mile out, French searchlights found *Walney* and seemingly every gun in port erupted. *Walney* charged into the maelstrom, ramming through both booms and into the claustrophobic harbor. In American-accented French a Royal Navy lieutenant futilely announced, "*Ne tirez pas. Nous sommes vos amis. Nous sommes les Américains.*" ("Do not fire. We are your friends. We are Americans.") Barely 100 yards abeam, moored French destroyers and submarines subjected *Walney* to point-blank fire as *Walney* passed their berths, physically mowing down *Walney*'s superstructure and slaughtering crew and soldiers who valiantly fought back as best they could. American and British bodies piled in heaps on deck. As Bennett predicted, *Reservist* had charged into a naval valley of death. *Walney* staggered through the gauntlet, somehow physically making her objective at the far end of the harbor without disintegrating. She was shortly a blazing, uncontrolled ghost ship; most of her complement were casualties.

Astern, *Hartland* was subjected to the same nightmare. French fire massacred all gun crews topside before she made port. As *Hartland* rounded the Môle Ravin Blanc to her objective, destroyer *Typhon* emptied her 130mm battery at a range of 100ft; several moored submarines also laid point-blank into *Hartland*, which lost power and began to burn. The defenders remorselessly kept pouring on the firepower. Men escaping the inferno below were cut down on deck. Ablaze and adrift, *Hartland* was abandoned at 0410hrs; the lifeless *Walney* blew up and capsized at 0445hrs.

Of 393 US Army personnel, 189 were killed, including Lieutenant-Colonel Marshall, posthumously awarded the Distinguished Service Cross and last seen hurling a grenade at *Walney*'s tormentors. An additional 157 US troops were wounded; just 47 survived unhurt to be captured. Royal Navy casualties were 113 killed and 86 wounded; the US Navy lost five killed and seven wounded. Total *Reservist* losses came to 307 killed and 250 wounded.

Captain Peters had been miraculously saved from his command's nighttime massacre by being physically blown off his own flagship. After surviving *Reservist*, Peters was cruelly killed in a plane crash a week later. He was posthumously awarded the Victoria Cross and the United States' Distinguished Service Medal.

Operation Villain, November 8

La Sénia and Tafaraoui airfields outside Oran were slated to be captured on D-Day by M3 Stuarts of Task Force Green. Clark, fearing unused American resources would get commandeered by the British, insisted on a

Operation *Villain*'s 2nd Battalion, 503rd Parachute Infantry Regiment trains at RAF Aldermaston with C-47s of the US 60th Troop Carrier Group, September 23, 1942. The 2nd/503rd PIR was redesignated the 2nd/509th PIR five days before *Villain*, on November 2. (US Air Force)

redundant parachute drop on the airfields to precede the tanks: Operation *Villain*. British planners opposed *Villain*, considering forces better used to reinforce the urgent offensive into Tunisia. Center Task Force's US Army planners felt *Villain* would make "no material difference" to the Oran operation; Eisenhower too was unimpressed. Colonel William Bentley (USAAF) commanded *Villain*'s "Parachute Task Force," comprising Lieutenant-Colonel Edson Raff's 556-man 2nd Battalion, 509th Parachute Infantry Regiment and the 39 C-47 Skytrains of Lieutenant-Colonel Thomas Schofield's USAAF 60th Troop Carrier Group.

Bentley's men studied two plans: Plan Peace and Plan War. On D-1 AFHQ would decide which to execute. If Plan Peace was in effect, the 2nd/509th PIR would depart in time to peacefully occupy La Sénia airfield in daylight on the morning of November 8. If Plan War was ordered, 2nd/509th PIR would take off four hours earlier and instead make a midnight combat drop on Tafaraoui. The ambiguity and suspense frustrated all; a 2nd/509th PIR sergeant snapped, "Are we supposed to go over there and fight or kiss our opponents?"

The flight plan was daunting. The C-47s were to depart southwest England, fly around Nazi-occupied France, then through unfriendly Spain and over the Mediterranean towards Algeria. After 1,500 miles in the dark, they were to arrive over Oran in sufficient order to secure the correct airfield. It would be the longest parachute drop of World War II, executed by a battalion of the US Army's embryonic airborne arm without combat experience.

Late on November 7, the paratroopers received word that Plan Peace had been declared. That night the Parachute Task Force's 39 C-47s departed from their Cornwall airfields. Immediately fog, darkness, and radio failures began to disrupt the mission. In mid-flight, unknown to the paratroopers, AFHQ scrapped Plan Peace and instituted Plan War. Off Oran, antiaircraft auxiliary HMS *Alynbank* was to guide the transports via homing signal broadcast at 440 kilocycles. Inexplicably, *Alynbank* broadcast at 460 kilocycles. Both *Alynbank*'s homing signal and desperate transmissions warning of the plan change went unheard by the Americans. After crossing into Spain, the C-47s climbed through the clouds to 10,000ft to overcome the coastal mountains. The transports became hopelessly lost, some diverging widely over the Western Mediterranean. Two C-47s landed in French Morocco; another made it to Gibraltar. One C-47 accidentally parachuted its charges over Spanish Morocco while another three C-47s landed there. Sixty-seven Americans would be interned by Franco's government. A fourth C-47 touched down amidst assumed friendly troops when its pilot, realizing the approaching soldiers were Spaniards, frantically took off again to avoid capture.

Low on fuel and morale, the 32 remaining C-47s crossed the Algerian coast at 0600hrs on D-Day. Unsure of their location, 12 C-47s dropped their men, including Raff, southeast of Lourmel. The landed paratroopers began making their way towards La Sénia airfield 35 miles to the northeast. Bentley's C-47 overflew La Sénia and was repulsed by French antiaircraft fire – the first notice that Plan Peace was scuttled. Near Oran three C-47s were forced down, their personnel, including Bentley, captured by local French police. Remaining C-47s began landing at the western end of Sebkha d'Oran at 0830hrs.

Beach X (Mersa bou Zedjar), November 8

The US 1st Armored Division's Combat Command A (CCA) had remained in Britain for further training, but its Combat Command B (CCB) would see extensive action in *Torch*. For D-Day, CCB/1A was divided into two Task Forces, Green and Red. Colonel Paul Robinett's Task Force Green, comprising one third of CCB/1A, would make the most westerly landing at Mersa bou Zedjar at Beach X. Under Robinett's command were assault troops, shore party, main body, and a "flying column" under Lieutenant-Colonel John Todd. Upon securing the beach head, Task Force Green's mission was to first secure the airstrip at Lourmel, then advance towards either Tafaraoui or La Sénia airfields.

The Center Task Force convoy assigned to Beach X comprised transports *Batory*, *Queen Emma*, *Princess Beatrix*, *Benalbenach*, *Mary Slessor*, *Mark Twain*, *Walt Whitman*, and Maracaibo LST *Bachaquero*. *Bachaquero* carried 20 M3 Stuart light tanks and other vehicles that were to be landed directly on the beach. Thirty-nine landing craft were available for ship-to-shore operations. US infantry would need a reliable method to identify unknown persons in the dark as friendly troops. Center Task Force's solution was smirkingly American: the challenger would cry out, "Hi-yo Silver!" Fellow GIs would respond, "Aw-aaaay!"

In the dark of H-Hour, a brightly lit Oran-bound convoy of five French merchantmen and an armed trawler suddenly interposed themselves between the Allied transports and Beach X. The Royal Navy boarded one vessel; the rest fled east towards Les Andalouses – directly into Center Task Force's Beach Y assault convoy. Now under attack by cruiser HMS *Aurora*, the French merchantmen reversed back west towards the Beach X flotilla, then grounded off Cap Figalo. The armed trawler escaped into the night. The episode delayed Beach X landings 35 minutes.

FAR LEFT
Anxious US troops of the Center Task Force hang tight in a British LCA as they await landfall near Oran. Royal Navy sailors pilot them ashore, while Royal Navy beach parties are awaiting them at the landing zones. Anecdotes of national friction on D-Day are relatively scarce. (World War II Today)

LEFT
A British transport transfers a US 37mm M3 antitank gun into a landing craft off Algeria. A half-track has already been loaded. In North Africa, American troops immediately found the 37mm M3 hopelessly inadequate against German armor. The 37mm began to be phased out in 1943, replaced by the British-designed 57mm M1. (IWM A 12685)

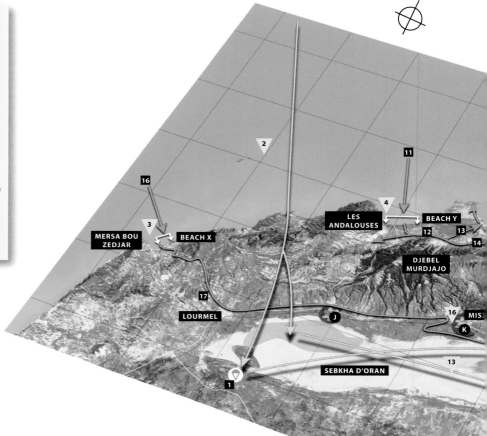

US UNITS

1. US 2nd/509th PIR (*Villain*)
2. US 1st Rangers

US 1st Infantry Division

3. US 16th Infantry RCT
4. 1st/16th RCT
5. 2nd/16th RCT
6. 3rd/16th RCT
7. US 18th Infantry RCT
8. 1st/18th RCT
9. 2nd/18th RCT
10. 3rd/18th RCT
11. US 26th Infantry RCT
12. 1st/26th RCT
13. 2nd/26th RCT
14. 3rd/26th RCT

US 1st Armored Division

15. *Reservist* task force (3rd/6th US Armored Infantry)
16. Task Force Green
17. Green flying column
18. Task Force Red
19. Red flying column
20. Planned C-47 landing zone

▼ EVENTS

Center Task Force, November 8

1. Peters' *Reservist* task force enters Oran Harbor at 0300hrs. Ferocious French resistance sinks both sloops HMS *Walney* and HMS *Hartland*. Allied casualties are severe and the French successfully sabotage the port.

2. Late on November 7, US 2nd/509 PIR departs UK in 39 C-47s to execute Operation *Villain*. Scattered and disorganized, none successfully reach La Sénia airfield. Twelve C-47s drop paratroopers south of Lourmel. Twenty-eight C-47s land at the Sebkha d'Oran at 0830hrs.

3. Robinett's Task Force Green lands at Beach X. Green flying column's 20 M3 Stuarts capture Lourmel's airfield by 1200hrs with little resistance.

4. Roosevelt's 26th RCT lands at Beach Y at 0045hrs.

5. Cheadle's 16th RCT lands at beaches Z White and Z Red at 0100hrs.

6. Greer's 18th RCT lands at Beach Z Green at 0120hrs and captures Arzew's naval base.

7. Oliver's Task Force Red lands at Beach Z Red at 0100hrs. At 0835hrs, Waters' Red flying column departs for Tafaraoui airfield.

8. Darby's 1st Rangers assaults Arzew, capturing Fort de la Pointe and Fort du Nord by 0400hrs.

9. French destroyers *Typhon*, *Tramontane*, and *Tornade* sortie from Oran at 0515hrs. Cruiser HMS *Aurora* sinks *Tramontane* and drives off *Tornade* which is beached. *La Surprise* opens fire on transport *Llangibby Castle* at 0645hrs and is sunk by destroyer HMS *Brilliant* at 0715hrs. By 1137hrs, HMS *Aurora* and cruiser HMS *Jamaica* drive *Typhon* back into Oran and recently sortied destroyer *Épervier* aground.

10. Waters' Red flying column captures Tafaraoui Airfield at 1112hrs. Twenty-six Spitfires of the USAAF 31st Fighter Group arrive at Tafaraoui from Gibraltar at 1600hrs.

11. The 1st/16th RCT is ambushed by elements of 2e RTA, but captures La Macta at 1330hrs.

12. At noon, 18th RCT begins its series of unsuccessful attacks against the fortified village of St Cloud.

13. The 509th PIR's Colonel Raff dispatches his landed C-47s to Tafaraoui. French fighters shoot down several C-47s en route.

Center Task Force, November 9

14. Shortly after 0600hrs, French armor counterattacks at St Lucien and most of Red flying column returns to defend Tafaraoui. By afternoon CCB/1A's Company B and a platoon of M3 75mm GMC tank destroyers drive the French from St Lucien, destroying 14 Char D1s with little loss.

15. Todd's Green flying column captures La Sénia airfield at 1000hrs.

16. Robinett's Task Force Green unsuccessfully attacks Misserrhin all day, then bypasses the town through the muddy Sebkha d'Oran on the night of November 9/10.

17. French infantry encircles and attacks 16th RCT but is hit by air strikes and driven back.

18. Roosevelt's 26th RCT advances through heavy French artillery fire and 600 troops of the 2e RZ to Bouisseville.

19. The 18th RCT resumes attacking St Cloud at 0700hrs, but Allen belays the planned artillery bombardment and further attacks. The 1st/18th RCT remains overnight to pin the French at St Cloud.

Center Task Force, November 10

20. The 2nd/16th RCT and 3rd/16th RCT fight the French I/2e RZ and 68e RAA at St Eugène and eventually force their surrender.

21. After bypassing St Cloud during the night, 3rd/18th RCT captures Pointe Canastel's coastal battery, while 2nd/18th RCT runs into II/2e RZ and 155mm guns of 66e RAA.

22. Battleship *Rodney* and 2nd/26th RCT attack Fort du Santon.

23. By 0900hrs, Task Forces Green and Red rendezvous south of Oran. Taking French fire, the task forces drive into the city. Negotiations for Oran's surrender begin at 1230hrs.

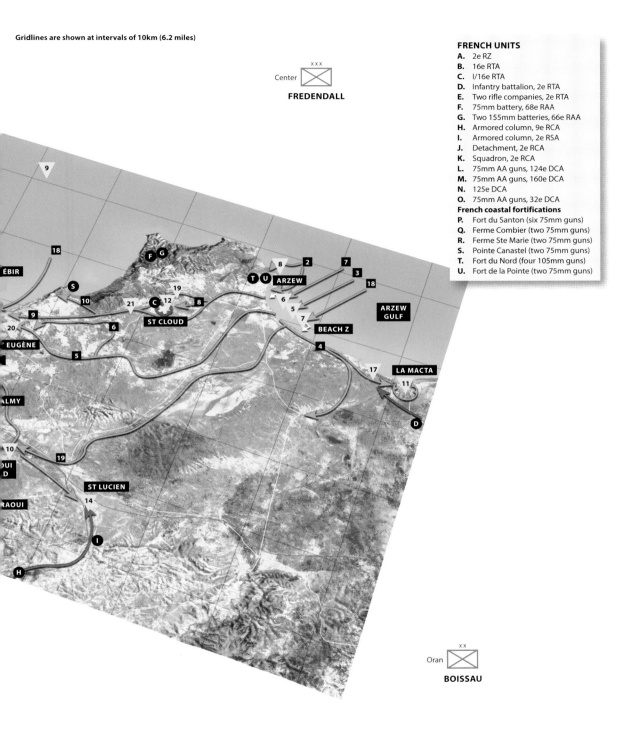

Gridlines are shown at intervals of 10km (6.2 miles)

FRENCH UNITS
- **A.** 2e RZ
- **B.** 16e RTA
- **C.** I/16e RTA
- **D.** Infantry battalion, 2e RTA
- **E.** Two rifle companies, 2e RTA
- **F.** 75mm battery, 68e RAA
- **G.** Two 155mm batteries, 66e RAA
- **H.** Armored column, 9e RCA
- **I.** Armored column, 2e RSA
- **J.** Detachment, 2e RCA
- **K.** Squadron, 2e RCA
- **L.** 75mm AA guns, 124e DCA
- **M.** 75mm AA guns, 160e DCA
- **N.** 125e DCA
- **O.** 75mm AA guns, 32e DCA

French coastal fortifications
- **P.** Fort du Santon (six 75mm guns)
- **Q.** Ferme Combier (two 75mm guns)
- **R.** Ferme Ste Marie (two 75mm guns)
- **S.** Pointe Canastel (two 75mm guns)
- **T.** Fort du Nord (four 105mm guns)
- **U.** Fort de la Pointe (two 75mm guns)

Center ××× FREDENDALL

ARZEW
ARZEW GULF
ST CLOUD
BEACH Z
LA MACTA
EUGÈNE
ST LUCIEN

Oran ×× BOISSAU

CENTER TASK FORCE LANDINGS AT ORAN, NOVEMBER 8–10, 1942

The US 1st Infantry Division and US 1st Armored Division's Combat Command B landed at Oran, supported by British naval gunfire and airpower. Despite the *Villain* mishap and *Reservist* disaster, Fredendall's Center Task Force overcame stiff French resistance and secured the *Torch* landings' only pure military victory.

Inbound to the beach, one of the landing craft caught fire and was abandoned. Long after the boat was scuttled, a fuel slick blazed, further disorganizing the landings; at Beach X Green the second assault wave landed first. *Bachaquero* ran aground on an unexpected sandbar, still 120 yards from shore. The 16th Armored Engineers spent the next three hours building a pontoon bridge that did not quite reach land. Numerous LCMs also beached in the shallows; bulldozers freed them but disabled ten in the process, leaving just three operational. Despite delays and difficulties, the armored Green flying column exited the beach for Lourmel at 0900hrs and brushed aside a French armored car to take the village and airfield. That afternoon CCB/1A's Brigadier-General Oliver dispatched the Green flying column to capture La Sénia airfield via the route north of the Sebkha d'Oran.

Beach Y (Les Andalouses), November 8

US 1st Infantry Division deputy Brigadier-General Teddy Roosevelt, Jr directly commanded 26th RCT, landing west of Oran. Roosevelt's target was Beach Y at Les Andalouses. While Aurora was engaging the French convoy at 2320hrs, Allied transports *Glengyle*, *Monarch of Bermuda*, *Llangibby Castle*, *Clan MacTaggart*, and *Salacia* disgorged their soldiers into 45 Royal Navy-crewed landing craft. Inexplicably *Monarch of Bermuda*'s ladder rungs were 2ft apart instead of the standard 1ft; heavily laden troops predictably took longer to board. The first assault wave from *Monarch of Bermuda* and *Glengyle* commenced their six-mile run to the beach at 2345hrs. An uncharted sandbar also plagued Beach Y. The first three LCMs from *Glengyle* ran aground, then disembarked heavy equipment that rolled forward a few yards and plunged underwater.

A captured French soldier is interrogated outside Oran by Americans of the Center Task Force. In three days' fighting, Allen's US 1st Infantry Division took 1,364 French prisoners. Most Allied personnel captured by the French during *Torch* were the product of the ill-advised *Terminal*, *Reservist*, and *Villain* raids. (US Army)

Eight LCPRs from *Llangibby Castle* landed 26th RCT's second wave at Y Green at 0138hrs. Miles distant aboard *Reina del Pacifico*, Major-General Terry Allen observed the flares announcing Roosevelt's first waves were ashore. Playing to morale, Allen announced, "Boys, I thought you'd like to know our first two waves landed without opposition." Then with a grin, "I've just sent a signal to the French to put in their first team!" Two hours later, 26th RCT's transports had closed to within 2,000 yards of the beach and by 0500hrs 26th RCT reported 2,670 men and 33 vehicles ashore at Y Green and Y White.

At 0515hrs, French destroyers *Typhon*, *Tramontane*, and *Tornade* escaped Oran's *Reservist*-wrecked harbor and engaged lurking HMS *Aurora*. The British cruiser sank *Tramontane* and drove off *Tornade* which was beached. French sloop *La Surprise* suddenly appeared at 0645hrs and opened fire on transport *Llangibby Castle*, anchored a mile off Les Andalouses. Destroyer HMS *Brilliant* raced to intercede, dueling *La Surprise* until the French vessel blew up and sank at 0715hrs, suffering 55 dead.

Coastal artillery at Fort du Stanton repeatedly hit transport *Llangibby Castle* at 0917hrs, compelling her to withdraw, then struck *Monarch of Bermuda* at 1050hrs. Counter-battery fire from *Rodney* temporarily discouraged the French guns but failed to destroy them. By 1137hrs, cruisers *Aurora* and *Jamaica* had driven *Typhon* back into port and recently sortied *Épervier* aground. Cunningham's after-action report quipped, "*Aurora* polished off her opponents with practiced ease."

Beach Z (Arzew), November 8

The strongest Center Task Force landings were at Golfe d'Arzew by most of Major-General Terry Allen's US 1st Infantry Division. They consisted of the 16th and 18th RCTs under Colonel Henry Cheadle and Colonel Frank Greer, and an attached force of Lieutenant-Colonel William Darby's 1st Rangers. They were joined by Task Force Red, the largest part of CCB/1A, under Brigadier-General Lunsford Oliver. Many GIs, irritated at their Royal Navy hosts and appalled at their food, were eager to depart the British transports. As H-Hour approached, some Americans soothed their nerves by listening to the Army–Notre Dame football game in New York, picked up on shortwave radio and broadcast live over intercom.

At sunrise, eight *Furious* Albacores and 12 Sea Hurricanes from *Dasher* and *Biter* took off. They raced to Valmy, dropped propaganda leaflets, then turned back towards La Sénia. In full daylight they ran into stiff antiaircraft fire and enemy fighters. The Albacores each dropped six 250lb bombs onto the airfield, destroying empty hangars. French Dw.250s knocked down three Albacores at the cost of five of their own. Several minutes later, ten *Furious* Seafires, in the type's combat debut, strafed French antiaircraft batteries and parked aircraft at La Sénia and Tafaraoui airfields. Royal Navy aircraft would maintain aggressive patrols throughout D-Day. Six *Formidable* Seafires shot down a snooping French DB-7 bomber over Mers-el-Kébir, then claimed four more Dw.520s. Several Seafires, low on fuel, were forced to land amongst friendly American forces in Algeria. With just 50 gallons left in his tanks, Sub-Lieutenant Peter Twiss offered to fly short reconnaissance missions for American troops. After crash-landing on D-Day, Sub-Lieutenant P. J. Hutton would make his way to Tafaraoui and the following day fly another sortie in a borrowed USAAF Spitfire.

Darby split his combined Anglo-American force into two detachments to complete their D-Day objectives. The first section of two companies departed *Royal Scotsman* for Arzew harbor. Achieving surprise, they overpowered two French sentries and secured Fort de la Pointe and the northern side of Arzew. Darby led the second detachment of four companies from *Royal Ulsterman* and *Royal Monarch*. The 1st Rangers landed southeast of Cap Carbon, scaled cliffs and infiltrated behind the main battery of four 105mm guns at Fort du Nord. Supported by 81mm mortars they attacked, losing two killed and eight wounded. At 0400hrs, Darby's green flare announced the Arzew battery was captured.

Colonel Cheadle's 16th RCT of 5,608 men had landed at beaches Z White and Z Red at 0100hrs. Cheadle's battalions prepared Beach Z Red for Task Force Red's later landing, then pushed aside light resistance to take several objectives ahead of schedule. Advance units at La Macta were ambushed by French troops from the 2e RTA. Supported by destroyer HMS *Farndale*'s naval gunfire, the Americans took La Macta at 1330hrs.

British sailors assist infantry of the US 18th RCT as they debark *Reina del Pacifico*. Waiting to take them to Oran's Beach Z Green is the Royal Navy's *LCA 28*. Swimming was impossible for assault troops weighed down with combat gear; an inadvertent stumble or careless moment while boarding was potentially fatal. (World War II Today)

Arzew, November 8, 1942. Rangers of the 1st Battalion guard the French coastal artillery battery they captured in the early dark of D-Day. Bullet damage from the preceding firefight is apparent. The modern Rangers were founded by future Goalpost commander Lucian Truscott in June 1942. Truscott and 50 Rangers participated in the Dieppe raid and were the first Americans to see ground combat against Nazi Germany. (US Army)

Colonel William Cheadle's 16th RCT lands at Z White Beach near St Leu on the morning of November 8, 1942. The following day, Cheadle's 1st Battalion gave the Center Task Force its most precarious moment when it was briefly besieged at La Macta. (US Army)

Colonel Greer's 7,092-strong 18th RCT had departed transports *Ettrick*, *Tegelberg*, and *Reina del Pacifico* and begun landing at Arzew's Beach Z Green at 0120hrs. Greer's 3rd Battalion captured the French barracks at Arzew, including 62 prisoners. Around 0600hrs, Major-General Allen departed *Reina del Pacifico* for shore; minutes later the transport was hit by French artillery. Shortly afterward, US officers broke into the Arzew town hall and compelled the terrified Vichyite mayor to surrender the town via telephone. They were aided by Edgar Hamilton, an American captain in the Foreign Legion who had immediately defected; Hamilton now dispensed valuable intelligence and tactical advice. With the help of a 60mm mortar barrage, 3rd/18th RCT captured the Arzew naval base, including 13 seaplanes fully fueled and armed with torpedoes.

Meanwhile, 1st Battalion, 18th RCT forged inland to seize St Cloud and the Djebel Khar hill to its west. Five French TBC armored cars attacked near Rénan and were destroyed by 37mm antitank guns. At 1200hrs, 18th RCT arrived at St Cloud, a village of 3,500, and the French suddenly gave a fierce account of themselves. Defending St Cloud were no fewer than 400 troops of the 16e RTA and a Foreign Legion battalion armed with 14 75mm guns, four 37mm guns, four 60mm mortars, and eight heavy and 15 light machine guns. At noon, vicious fire repulsed the first American attack, while batteries of the 66e RAA and 68e RAA perched on heights to the northwest bombarded the Americans with 75mm and 155mm fire. Reinforced by 2nd Battalion, 18th RCT and 105mm assault guns of the 18th's cannon company, the Americans attacked at 1530hrs and were again repelled. Late that afternoon, 3rd/168th RCT arrived from Arzew, and a third attack was planned for 0700hrs, November 9.

At 0400hrs that morning, Brigadier-General Oliver's 4,772-strong Task Force Red had landed at Beach Z Red from the transports *Durban Castle* and *Derbyshire* and LSTs *Misoa* and *Tasajera*. Under fire from a French battery at St Leu, all were fully disembarked at 0759hrs. A flying column of M3 Stuarts and armored infantry under Patton's son-in-law, Lieutenant-Colonel John Waters, exited the beach at 0835hrs. Fighting through light resistance, Waters attacked Tafaraoui airfield at 1112hrs and quickly captured the airstrip, 300 French prisoners, and an approaching ammunition train. French bombers from La Sénia attacked Tafaraoui, but Royal Navy fighters repelled them, shooting down four and losing one. At 1600hrs, 26 Spitfires of the USAAF 31st Fighter Group arrived at Tafaraoui from Gibraltar, mistaking four French Dw.250s for an expected flight of Sea Hurricanes. The French fighters shot down the first unassuming Spitfire on its landing approach; in the ensuing mêlée, the Americans downed all four Dewoitines without further loss.

Twenty miles west, Lieutenant-Colonel Raff dispatched his landed C-47s to Tafaraoui airfield. French fighters from La Sénia jumped and shot down several transports. The survivors were greeted at

US troops and Royal Navy shore parties of the Center Task Force unload *LCA 26* in the Arzew surf. The Royal Navy's doctrine of bringing assault transports very close to shore is demonstrated here. French artillery struck several Center Task Force transports. (US Army)

Tafaraoui by a French 75mm artillery barrage from nearby hills. By dusk, just 14 C-47s remained operational. Casualties and general chaos had reduced Raff's original complement of 556 men to just 300 available for further operations. The same French air and artillery attacks frustrated Waters' desire to advance towards La Sénia that afternoon; the delay allowed additional Task Force Red elements to reinforce him overnight. Waters set out for La Sénia at 0600hrs the following morning, November 9.

End run to Oran, November 9–10

Strong French counterstrokes developed on D+1. At Les Andalouses, Roosevelt's 26th RCT weathered an assault against Beach Y, then advanced slowly towards Mers-el-Kébir, slogging through heavy French artillery fire and 600 troops of 2e RZ. Meanwhile French armor counterattacked at St Lucien, seven miles southeast of Tafaraoui airfield. North of Tafaraoui a reinforced tank company continued towards La Sénia airfield under French artillery fire, but the rest of the Red flying column about-faced to defend the threatened Tafaraoui airdrome. A reconnaissance platoon from 1st Battalion, 1st Armored Regiment pinned the French. That afternoon, 1st Armored's Company B and a platoon of M3 75mm GMC tank destroyers departed Tafaraoui airfield and drove the French from St Lucien, destroying 14 Char D1 light tanks while losing one killed, an M3 Stuart, and an M3 GMC.

The most serious threat developed farthest east. A battalion of French infantry had skillfully approached overnight and encircled the 1st/16th RCT at La Macta, threatening Beach Z and prompting an onsite naval fire support officer to proclaim the situation "horrible." Center Task Force diverted major forces and prepared a naval bombardment to save the left flank, radioing, "Help coming: tanks, engineers, bombers, Spitfires." Air strikes and 1st/16th RCT repulsed the French before most Allied reinforcements arrived.

Meanwhile, Todd's Green flying column reached La Sénia airfield at dawn, capturing it without loss at 1000hrs. Most French aircraft had already fled; Todd's haul came to 159 prisoners, 61 rifles, and four machine guns. French 75mm batteries near Valmy heavily shelled the airfield but were expelled by a Green detachment that evening.

Robinett's Task Force Green, minus Todd's flying column, had arrived at Misserrhin that morning, facing French machine-gun bunkers, armored cars, and a 75mm battery above. A frontal attack by M3 Stuarts at 1030hrs failed, as did a flanking attempt. Short of infantry, Robinett waited until night to bypass Misserrhin to the south. In the dark the Americans accidentally entered the muddy Sebkha d'Oran and discovered it was passable by vehicles after all.

Colonel Greer's 18th RCT had commenced its direct assault on St Cloud at 0700hrs, November 9, but quickly stalled due to ferocious French resistance, taking serious casualties. Greer planned a new attack, preceded by a devastating artillery bombardment on the town, followed by all three infantry battalions. Concerned over civilian casualties, Major-General Allen belayed the order, halting all US artillery fire on the town. The 1st/18th RCT would fix the

The Royal Navy's Force H cruises off Algeria during Operation *Torch*. In frame are battleships HMS *Duke of York* and HMS *Rodney*, battlecruiser HMS *Renown*, fleet carrier HMS *Formidable*, and light cruiser HMS *Argonaut*. In the end no major Italian naval units sortied to interfere with the *Torch* landings. (IWM A 012958)

HMS *Formidable*'s Captain A. G. Talbot and two junior officers view the Algerian coast through binoculars, November 1942. The focus of the officers' attention may have been US ground forces making the final attack into Oran on the morning of November 10. (World War II Database)

French while 2nd/18th and 3rd/18th would bypass St Cloud that night. Meanwhile, Allen's commanders met to plan a set-piece attack on Oran the following morning. Supported by divisional artillery, Oran would be encircled from the northwest by all three battalions of Roosevelt's 26th RCT, which had advanced through stout French resistance on the Plaine des Andalouses, and from the east by five battalions of the 16th and 18th RCTs. Task Forces Green and Red would converge south of Oran and provide the main armored thrust into the city.

The night of November 9/10 saw the exhausted troops of 16th and 18th RCTs marching into position to envelop Oran. The 3rd Battalion, 16th RCT had closed unnoticed to the city's outskirts and was preparing to attack when Allen's orders were received; the 3rd/16th RCT was compelled to actually withdraw to the designated line of departure. In the process they ran into 2nd/16th RCT, caught in a stiff firefight near St Eugène with the French 1st Battalion of the 2e RZ and the 68e RAA. A few hours later the French surrendered. Meanwhile trucks brought 1st/16th RCT from La Macta to join 2nd/16th RCT and 3rd/16th RCT outside Oran.

The 18th RCT's 2nd and 3rd battalions had successfully bypassed St Cloud during the night but were delayed by French resistance along the coast and inland. Supported by the 32nd Field Artillery Battalion, 3rd/18th RCT took Pointe Canastel's coastal battery. Hours behind, 2nd/18th RCT ran into the now-alert French 2nd Battalion of the 2e RZ and 155mm guns of the 66e RAA. Neither US battalion would reach the perimeter in time for the coordinated assault on Oran.

As dawn broke on November 10, battleship *Rodney* and cruisers *Jamaica* and *Aurora* stood by to provide fire support while Force H closed to facilitate carrier strikes. Task Forces Green and Red rendezvoused south of Oran and were shelled by French 75mm guns at Valmy; with difficulty and naval fire support, they overcame the French and were ready to attack Oran by 0900hrs. The recombined CCB/1A pushed through initial fire into the strangely quiet city. Armored columns thrust directly for Général de division Boissau's headquarters and seized the port and other key locations. Allen canceled the planned artillery and aerial attacks. Boissau and Vice-Amiral Rioult began negotiating the formal surrender of Oran at 1230hrs. Again, terms were lenient. Allied and French prisoners were exchanged. Fighting inadvertently continued outside the city. As late as 1330hrs, Fort du Santon was still under attack by 26th RCT and battleship *Rodney*. The 1st/18th RCT had attacked St Cloud that morning and been repeatedly thrown back before the French surrendered the town on Boissau's order. St Cloud's capitulation ended French resistance near Oran. Center Task Force had suffered 1,189 casualties, including 593 killed and missing. French losses were 700, with 347 killed and missing.

WESTERN TASK FORCE

French Morocco, established in 1912, claimed 6.3 million inhabitants. Mountainous inland, Morocco possesses an Atlantic coast poor in harbors and pounded by intense surf. Patton's objective was cosmopolitan Casablanca, population 257,000 and described by a *Torch* planner as "half Arabian, half European, and half Hollywood."

The 33,843-strong all-American Western Task Force would execute a three-pronged assault on French Morocco. The main offensive, comprising most of Patton's infantry, would land 18 miles up the coast at the resort town of Fedala to envelop Casablanca from landwards. Ninety miles north, a separate landing would secure Mehdia-Port Lyautey's all-weather airfield. The third landing would seize Safi, 140 miles south of Casablanca. Patton's 55 M4 Shermans, too large for existing tank lighters, would unload at Safi's deepwater harbor.

Battling Morocco's notorious Atlantic surf, Brushwood invasion waves charge towards the Fedala coast. On the far left is an LCPR, immediately to its right is an LCM. The tension and focus on the young coxswains' faces is apparent. A year ago they might have been in high school. (US Navy)

French forces defending Morocco were divided into four divisions plus coastal and air defenses comprising 55,000 troops, over 120 tanks, and 80 armored cars. Air strength consisted of 40 Dw.250 and 46 Hawk 75 fighters, 39 Le0 451 and 26 DB-7 bombers, and 13 Po 63.11 reconnaissance aircraft based at Marrakech, Rabat-Salé, Meknès, Agadir, and Casablanca.

Prior to sailing, the joint commanders of Western Task Force had met and briefed their counterparts on the mission. With French belligerency uncertain, a communications system was needed to address rules of engagement. In the event an American unit was fired on by the French, it would report, "Batter up!" If permission was granted to retaliate, Task Force 34 would respond, "Play ball!" As at Oran, US troops devised a nighttime call-and-response to identify friendly troops in the dark, gleefully conceiving the challenge "George!" and response "Patton!"

Sub-Task Force Brushwood landings at Fedala, November 8

Fedala's approaches were defended by Batterie de Pont Blondin's three 138mm M1910 guns at Sherki, and Batterie de Fedala's three 100mm M1897/1910s and two 75mm guns at Cap de Fedala, all well placed on promontories offering enfilading fire of the beaches. Before sailing, TG 34.9 commander Captain Robert Emmet had observed, "It would be worth two destroyers to knock those guns out." Comprising Fedala's maneuver strength were three Renault FT tanks, about 100 Senegalese *tirailleurs* of the 6e RTS' 102e Défense Côtière (coastal defense) Company, and the 53e Défense Contre Avions (DCA)'s four 105mm guns. Dominating Casablanca was the powerful Batterie d'El Hank's four 194mm M1902 guns and four 138mm M1910s. Four more 100mm M1897/1910s and two 75mms rounded out Casablanca's coastal artillery.

Fleet carrier *Ranger* and auxiliary carrier *Suwannee* would fly air support for the Fedala area with 77 F4F Wildcats and 27 SBD Dauntlesses and TBF Avengers. Heavy cruiser *Augusta*, light cruiser *Brooklyn*, and four destroyers would provide naval fire support.

Late on November 7, the Center Attack Group arrived off Fedala. Assembling six miles offshore, the 12 transports and three cargo ships dropped anchor at midnight. On board were 19,870 US Army troops, 1,701

Western Task Force landings in Morocco, November 8–11, 1942.

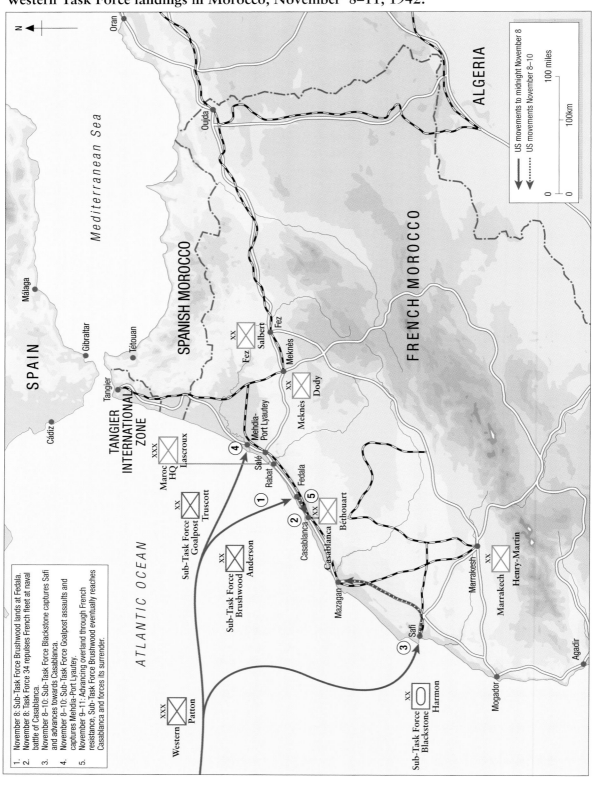

1. November 8: Sub-Task Force Brushwood lands at Fedala.
2. November 8: Task Force 34 repulses French fleet at naval battle of Casablanca.
3. November 8–10: Sub-Task Force Blackstone captures Safi and advances towards Casablanca.
4. November 8–10: Sub-Task Force Goalpost assaults and captures Mehdia-Port Lyautey.
5. November 9–11: Advancing overland through French resistance, Sub-Task Force Brushwood eventually reaches Casablanca and forces its surrender.

vehicles, and 15,000 tons of supplies. The initial assault wave of four battalion landing teams (BLTs) debarked from transports *Leonard Wood*, *Thomas Jefferson*, *Charles Carroll*, and *Joseph T. Dickman*. Designated BLT 1-7, BLT 2-7, BLT 1-30, and BLT 2-30, each landing team required over 40 LCPRs and up to nine LCVs, requiring BLTs to borrow landing craft from transports astern. The four control destroyers *Wilkes*, *Swanson*, *Ludlow*, and *Murphy* assembled 4,000 yards offshore, each leading a BLT's landing craft to its beach.

Minutes before H-Hour, the destroyer *Wilkes* blinkered, "The Yanks are coming!" but the 0400hrs assault was delayed; the first waves came ashore at 0515hrs. General confusion and an ebb tide played havoc with the landings. Scores of boats were wrecked and some heavily equipped troops drowned. Units were scattered and deposited miles from their actual beach. Task Force 34 would lose 160 out of 347 landing craft at Fedala, mostly on D-Day, permanently affecting later operations.

At 0520hrs, French searchlights flashed on and were promptly shot out by an American armed support boat. Faint dawn arrived at 0600hrs followed by machine-gun and coastal-battery fire at the invasion fleet from Cap Fedala and Sherki. The four control destroyers proceeded to their fire control stations, *Wilkes* announcing, "Batter up!" Long before receiving "Play ball!" at 0620hrs, *Murphy* and *Ludlow* returned fire on Sherki, *Wilkes* and *Swanson* on Cap Fedala. Light cruiser *Brooklyn* added her 6in. battery to the din at 0622hrs. *Murphy* had closed to 5,000 yards when Batterie du Pont Blondin struck the destroyer in the starboard engine room, killing three. Ashore, BLT 2-30 and elements of BLT 2-7 rallied to attack the battery. Damaged by 81mm mortars and 10,000-yard fire from *Brooklyn*, Batterie du Pont Blondin surrendered to the US infantry's improvised assault at 0730hrs.

Despite landing difficulties, BLT 1-7 had secured Fedala by 0600hrs, capturing the German Armistice Commission. Under fire, BLT 1-7 would seize a heavy antiaircraft battery by 1100hrs. Meanwhile, BLT 1-30 had landed at Blue Beach and at 0700hrs ambushed a train, taking 75 French troops prisoner.

Heavy cruiser *Augusta* had begun engaging Batterie de Fedala at 0710hrs. Batterie du Port opened on the invasion fleet an hour later, intermittently discouraged by naval fire. At 0835hrs, US troops ashore relayed, "For Christ's sake quit firing – you are killing our own troops! This is from Army – you are killing townspeople, no opposition ashore. If you quit firing they will surrender." At noon, a combined-arms assault captured Batterie de Fedala's 100mm guns and 22 prisoners. Under fire from American mortars and 75mm pack howitzers, Cap Fedala's 75mm guns and machine-gun bunkers surrendered at 1500hrs.

The naval battle of Casablanca, November 8

Thirty miles northwest of Casablanca, carrier USS *Ranger* had launched her first Wildcats at 0615hrs. Throughout D-Day, Wildcats would strafe French batteries and parked

Captured German Armistice Commission officers await American instructions at Fedala, November 8, 1942. Their bemused expressions appear to display incredulity at their sudden change in fortune. On any other day a cushy Armistice Commission assignment must have seemed far preferable to being stationed on the Eastern Front. (US Army)

Patton, eager to get ashore, viewed from the flagship *Augusta*. On D-Day *Augusta*'s first salvo blew the general's empty launch into the sea. A furious Patton lost all his kit; fortunately, minutes earlier an aide had managed to retrieve his prized ivory-handled revolvers. "Old Blood and Guts" seemed amused by his first sea battle, refusing to clean the yellow dye from his uniform when drenched by a French near-miss, but claimed naval combat seemed "kind of impersonal." (World War II Database)

USS *Ranger* (CV-4) launches her air group off Casablanca, November 8, 1942. Commissioned in 1934, the US Navy considered *Ranger* too small and too slow (29.5 knots) for the Pacific. *Ranger* fought just one other combat action, on October 4, 1943 while participating in Operation *Leader*. Operating with Britain's Home Fleet, *Ranger* struck German shipping and airfields at Bodø, Norway, making her the only US fleet carrier to engage German forces in World War II. (Navsource)

Viewed from destroyer USS *Mayrant* (DD-402) and flying two large battle ensigns, the brand-new South Dakota-class battleship USS *Massachusetts* (BB-59) maneuvers aggressively during the naval battle of Casablanca, November 8, 1942. Boasting nine 16in. guns and a top speed of 27 knots, "Big Mamie" was Task Force 34's insurance against a surprise appearance from the French battleship *Richelieu*. (Navsource)

aircraft at Rabat-Salé and Les Cazes airfields; Dauntlesses would provide air support ashore and dive-bomb French warships. By November 11, Task Force 34's 172 carrier aircraft would fly 1,078 sorties from four carriers and lose 44 aircraft to all causes.

At 0630hrs, the Covering Group's battleship *Massachusetts*, heavy cruisers *Wichita* and *Tuscaloosa*, and four destroyers turned in towards Casablanca at 25 knots – 18,000 yards to the coastal batteries at El Hank, 20,000 yards to the moored battleship *Jean Bart*. At 0701hrs, Batterie d'El Hank *and Jean Bart*'s single operational 380mm (15in.) turret opened on the Americans. El Hank's first salvo straddled *Massachusetts* and *Jean Bart*'s fell 600 yards short. Rear Admiral Giffen ordered, "Play ball!" and at 0704hrs, *Massachusetts*' 16in. main battery retaliated. The US Navy's only Atlantic fleet action of the 20th century was underway. Riding light cruiser *Brooklyn*, Morison described the battle as "an old-fashioned fire-away Flannigan." Here at Casablanca the French would provide the Atlantic theater's fiercest naval resistance to an Allied amphibious operation, including World War II's only instance of hostile warships bringing invading American landing craft under fire.

Massachusetts and *Tuscaloosa* ranged on *Jean Bart* while *Wichita* dueled the coastal battery at El Hank. *Massachusetts* unleashed nine salvoes, scoring five hits on the French battleship. *Massachusetts*' fifth hit at 0725hrs knocked out *Jean Bart*'s main battery. *Wichita* had quieted El Hank at 0727hrs and joined *Tuscaloosa* in bombarding Casablanca's submarine pen. By 0745hrs, US naval aircraft and gunfire had wrecked Casablanca's harbor, sinking three merchantmen and the submarines *Oréade*, *La Psyché*, and *Amphitrite*. Yet Giffen's Covering Group had been diverted west and at 0815hrs, Casablanca's Vice-Amiral Michelier dispatched seven French destroyers on a northeasterly end run to the US transports up the coast off Fedala: two 2,500-ton destroyers, *Milan* and *Albatros*, and five 1,400-tonners, *L'Alcyon*, *Brestois*, *Boulonnais*, *Fougueux*, and *Frondeur*. Eight French submarines sortied by 0830hrs, at which time the French destroyers had already opened fire on US landing craft en route to Fedala's Beach Yellow. They scored a direct hit on one US landing craft and engaged the US destroyers *Wilkes* and *Ludlow* several miles west of Cap Fedala. *Ludlow* set *Milan* afire before being struck herself at 0834hrs and knocked out of the battle for three hours. Both US destroyers fled towards the American cruisers. The US transports imperiled, Rear Admiral Hewitt ordered heavy cruiser *Augusta*, light cruiser *Brooklyn*, and destroyers *Wilkes* and *Swanson* to counterattack.

By 0848hrs the French destroyers had closed to within just four miles of the hapless US transports when *Augusta*, *Brooklyn*, *Wilkes*, and *Swanson* opened fire at 18,500 yards; an officer aboard a transport called the charging American warships "the most beautiful sight he ever saw." By 0900hrs, the French withdrew toward Casablanca's coastal

guns; they had caused a fright but no hits. They were now joined by French 7,300-ton cruiser *Primauguet*. Simultaneously, Hewitt ordered Giffen's Covering Group to neutralize the French; making 27 knots, they opened up from 19,400 yards at 0918hrs. *Augusta* and *Brooklyn* returned to the transports. The French warships skillfully used smoke screens in shoot-and-run feints, but at 1000hrs, two destroyers broke north to make torpedo runs at the Covering Group. Eleven miles distant *Massachusetts* and *Tuscaloosa* each scored against destroyer *Fougueux* which exploded and sank six and a half miles north of Casablanca. Almost simultaneously, *Massachusetts* was hit forward by a shell from El Hank, recording no casualties. Within three minutes, *Massachusetts* just threaded four French torpedoes, one by 15ft. Moments later, submarine *Médusa*'s four torpedoes barely missed *Tuscaloosa*.

The battleship USS *Massachusetts*' antiaircraft fire drives off four French fighters harassing a US spotter plane on the morning of November 8, 1942. Two weeks earlier in the South Pacific, *Massachusetts*' sister ship *South Dakota* shot down a record 26 enemy aircraft in a single day. (Navsource)

The Covering Group had again been lured west and three French destroyers made once more for the transports. At 0951hrs, Hewitt again ordered his two cruisers and three destroyers to intercept. *Brooklyn* just evaded five torpedoes from submarine *Amazone*; shortly thereafter, *Primauguet* and the six surviving French destroyers re-engaged US cruisers *Augusta*, *Brooklyn*, and destroyers *Wilkes*, *Swanson*, and *Bristol*. At 1046hrs, *Brooklyn* suffered her only hit, a dud. At 1100hrs, the Covering Group charged back over the western horizon, minus *Massachusetts*. With 60 percent of 16in. ammunition already expended, Giffen chose to withdraw his battleship in case *Richelieu* sortied from Dakar.

However, within minutes US warships badly damaged *Primauguet*, *Milan*, and *Brestois*; the French fled towards Casablanca. *Brestois* was further strafed by planes from *Ranger*; she foundered that evening. Under fire from El Hank, *Brooklyn* hit and sank *Boulannais* at 1112hrs. A few minutes later, French destroyers *Albatros*, *Frondeur*, and *L'Alcyon* formed up for a torpedo attack but were disrupted by fire from *Tuscaloosa* and *Wichita*. At 1128hrs, El Hank scored on *Wichita*; the heavy cruiser suffered 14 wounded. Ten minutes later *Wichita* evaded three torpedoes from a French submarine. American gunfire struck *Frondeur*, driving her back to Casablanca where she was strafed by *Ranger* aircraft. *Albatros* suffered three shell hits before being immobilized by two bombs from *Ranger* Dauntlesses.

A noontime lull was broken at 1245hrs by the sortie of sloop *La Grandière* and minesweepers *La Gracieuse* and *Commandant Delage* towards the US transports. A Dauntless bombed *La Grandière* and the three

Photographed from the flagship USS *Augusta* (CA-31), shells from Casablanca's El Hank battery miss the Benham-class destroyer USS *Mayrant* (DD-402) the morning of November 8, 1942. Among those later singled out for praise was a *Mayrant* gunnery officer, Lieutenant Franklin D. Roosevelt, Jr, USNR. (Navsource)

JEAN BART AT CASABLANCA, NOVEMBER 8, 1942 (PP. 56–57)

World War II saw nine battleship/battlecruiser gunnery duels, the most obscure at Casablanca between USS *Massachusetts* and the French *Jean Bart* on the morning of November 8, 1942, seen here. *Jean Bart*'s presence at Casablanca was well known to the US Navy, which considered her four 15in. guns the most immediate threat to a successful landing and gave her disabling top priority.

Jean Bart (**1**) opened fire on the Americans at 0701hrs, her yellow-dyed shells missing *Massachusetts* by 600 yards. *Massachusetts* unleashed the first of her three- to six-gun salvoes at 0704hrs. Moored at a known location, *Jean Bart* was an easy target; *Massachusetts*' first hit registered within two minutes. The American "super-heavy" 2,700lb 16in. shell smashed through two armored decks in *Jean Bart*'s stern and detonated in her empty 152mm magazine.

Massachusetts connected again at 0718hrs; the shell was a dud. *Jean Bart* continued to return fire. From 0728hrs to 0731hrs, two more 16in. shells struck underwater, ripping *Jean Bart* open to the sea, and a third 16in. round tore through *Jean Bart*'s funnel, two decks, and a bulkhead before exiting the battleship.

By 0733hrs, *Jean Bart* had fallen silent. The blazing harbor obscured targeting. *Massachusetts* ceased firing after her 13th salvo, then resumed at 0741hrs. Two 16in. duds struck *Jean Bart* again at 0759hrs, one jamming *Jean Bart*'s single operational turret before ricocheting into Casablanca, the second bouncing off *Jean Bart*'s second turret barbette. Minutes later, another 16in. shell exploded in *Jean Bart*'s starboard stern. The Americans ceased fire at 0828hrs. *Massachusetts* had delivered five direct hits and two damaging misses to *Jean Bart*, yet the American 16in. shells proved disturbingly defective.

Over the next several days, the French quietly repaired *Jean Bart*'s jammed turret, leaving the turret immobile as if still disabled. As Patton advanced on Casablanca near midday, November 10, *Jean Bart* awaited the perfect moment to strike. As USS *Augusta* unwittingly wandered into range, *Jean Bart*'s gunnery officer playfully beckoned the cruiser with his finger. Twin yellow geysers suddenly erupted in front of Hewitt's flagship, drenching her bridge. *Jean Bart*'s two-gun salvoes chased the fleeing *Augusta* until 1600hrs when nine Ranger Dauntlesses disabled *Jean Bart* with two 1,000lb bombs. Since D-Day, Jean Bart had fired 25 main battery rounds and suffered 22 dead.

vessels withdrew. That afternoon, *Ranger*'s air group savaged *Primauguet*, demolishing the cruiser and killing 29 bridge crew. El Hank defied naval fire and dive-bombing attacks all afternoon, eventually driving off *Wichita* and *Tuscaloosa* at 1450hrs. American D-Day air superiority was tenuous. *Ranger*'s VF-41 shot down seven Hawk 75s and destroyed five DB-7s on the ground, but couldn't stop French aircraft from strafing the beaches.

D-Day logistics were hobbled by landing craft attrition and overly front-loading assault transports with combat equipment. Some 15,000 tons of supplies languished offshore, while at best 1,000 tons a day could be unloaded at Fedala. By 1700hrs, just 16 percent of vehicles and 1.1 percent of supplies were ashore.

Sub-Task Force Blackstone assault at Safi, November 8–10

Safi, 140 miles south of Casablanca, was a phosphate-exporting town of 25,000 possessing a small but deep artificial harbor. Guarding Safi's coast were four 130mm M1924 guns of the Batterie de la Railleuse, and two 75mm guns of the Batterie du Port. Fewer than 1,000 French defended Safi, but they included 15 light tanks and five armored cars. A further 3,400 troops, 30 tanks, ten armored cars, and two battalions of horse-drawn artillery in Marrakech were half a day away.

Major-General Ernest Harmon of the 2nd Armored Division commanded the 6,428-strong Sub-Task Force Blackstone, Southern Attack Group's ground element. At daybreak November 7, the Southern Attack Group departed Task Force 34 for Safi. Riding light cruiser *Philadelphia*, Rear Admiral Lyal Davidson commanded battleship *New York*, auxiliary carrier *Santee*, eight destroyers, transports *Harris*, *Lyon*, *Calvert*, *Dorothea L. Dix*, seatrain *Lakehurst*, and numerous supporting vessels. That afternoon, *Lyon* transferred 350 assault troops onto destroyers *Bernadou* and *Cole*. The convoy arrived eight miles off Safi just before midnight.

Blackstone's harbor attack sortied towards Safi at 0345hrs, November 8. *Bernadou* penetrated Safi at 0428hrs and the French port erupted with 155mm, 75mm, machine-gun, and star-shell fire. *Bernadou*'s 3in. and 20mm guns retaliated; two 3in. shells silenced fire from the old Portuguese fortress atop the bluffs above. At 0430hrs, *Bernadou* docked and disgorged Company K, 47th Infantry Regiment. *Cole* moored and unloaded Company L at 0545hrs. By morning, the companies had won Safi's critical points from Foreign Legion defenders.

The first three waves of infantry and one wave of M5 Stuarts surged towards the Safi beaches at 0400hrs, escorted by destroyers *Mervine* and *Beatty*. Observing French fire, *Mervine* signaled "Batter up!" at 0428hrs; neither *Mervine*'s nor *Beatty*'s gunners waited for Admiral Davidson's "Play ball!" ten minutes later. At 0445hrs, the first troops of Major Frederic Feil's 1st BLT, 47th Infantry Regiment landed at Green Beach. Within 45 minutes, more than 600 men were ashore at Red, Blue, and Green beaches and were trading fire with French defenders. As day broke, naval gunfire support became

The destroyer USS *Bernadou* stripped down for Blackstone's Safi harbor strike, November 1942. In 1921, *Bernadou*'s sister USS *Cole* had achieved 41.2 knots and was ranked the fastest ship in the world, but by 1942 the two four-pipers' best days were behind them. (Navsource)

USS *Lakehurst* (APM-1) embarks a damaged floatplane at Safi after French hostilities ceased. SS *Seatrain New Jersey* was originally a railroad train ferry for Seatrain Lines' route between New York and Texas City, Texas. Requisitioned by the US Navy for *Torch*, USS *Lakehurst* was turned over to the US Army on August 2, 1943, becoming USAT *Lakehurst*. She was scrapped in 1973. (US Army)

more effective. Battleship *New York* knocked out Batterie Railleuse at 0850hrs and *Philadelphia*'s Curtiss SOC Seagull floatplanes bombed a 155mm battery.

The Armored Landing Team debarked from transports *Titania* and *Calvert* at 0900hrs. By 1000hrs, a platoon of M5 light tanks had secured Green Beach, while 1st BLT captured Front de Mer. As the French and US Navy traded salvoes, more than 1,000 members of 1st BLT had landed by midmorning. They were eventually joined ashore by 2nd BLT at Yellow Beach and 3rd BLT at Green Beach. By 1045hrs, all French batteries had been silenced. Another platoon of five M5 Stuarts from Blue Beach reinforced infantry finishing off French resistance at the Portuguese fortress. By afternoon, Blackstone had established a lodgment six miles deep. Seatrain USS *Lakehurst* arrived in harbor to unload her 55 M4 Sherman medium tanks, followed by *Titania*. *Lakehurst* immediately suffered a jammed derrick, delaying Sherman unloading five hours.

At 1350hrs the following day, November 9, *Santee* Wildcats spotted a reinforcing column from Marrakech and destroyed 14 trucks of the II/2e RTM, 2e REI, and 11e RCA. A few hours later, seven Dauntlesses and three Wildcats struck the Marrakech airfield, disabling 26 aircraft, then strafed 20 trucks from the earlier convoy. At 1700hrs, the Armored Landing Team engaged the French at Bou Gedra. Fighting continued the following morning, but Harmon intended to bypass local defenders. At 0900hrs, November 10, 2nd Armored Division's CCB set out for Casablanca. Destroyer *Cole* transported gasoline to Mazagan to refuel the CCB/2A Shermans en route.

Blackstone had suffered ten killed and 75 wounded, the US Navy just two casualties. Rushed into action, brand-new carrier USS *Santee* lost 21 of her 31 aircraft by November 11, none to actual combat.

Sub-Task Force Goalpost assault at Mehdia-Port Lyautey, November 8–10

Northern Attack Group's target was the all-weather airport at Port Lyautey, 90 miles north of Casablanca. The airstrip was five miles inland, nine miles navigating up the looping "U" of the Sebou River. A mile from the mouth was the village of Mehdia. High atop the river bluffs was the Kasbah, a formidable 16th-century Portuguese stone fortress. About 3,080 French infantry of the 1er RTM defended Port Lyautey, with 1,200 mechanized cavalry troops and 45 light tanks hours away in Rabat and 6,200 infantry five days distant in Rabat and Meknès. Mehdia-Port Lyautey would prove the most complicated of the Western Task Force landings. A *Torch* planner had despaired, "It would be hard to pick out a more difficult place to assault in all of West Africa."

Northern Attack Group's ground force was codenamed Sub-Task Force Goalpost. Major-General Lucian Truscott commanded 9,079 officers and men, 65 M5 Stuart light tanks, and 881 vehicles crammed aboard eight transports. Naval support was provided by auxiliary carrier *Sangamon*'s 12 Wildcats, nine Dauntlesses, and nine Avengers, along with battleship *Texas*, light cruiser *Savannah*, and seven destroyers.

Goalpost was to seize Port Lyautey's airport early on D-Day for Brigadier-General John Cannon's XII Air Support Command. Then 77 P-40s of 33rd Fighter Group would launch from auxiliary carrier *Chenango* on a one-way flight to base at Port Lyautey. Further XII Air Support Command elements would arrive as soon as possible from Gibraltar. The next objective was to capture the Salé airport near Rabat; if the French still refused to cooperate, Goalpost would lead the Western Task Force drive into Algeria.

The Northern Attack Group arrived 15,000 yards off Mehdia at midnight, November 7–8. Three battalion landing teams would hit five beaches across ten miles of Mehdia-Port Lyautey's coastline. Perfect transatlantic navigation was ruined by last-minute maneuvering, wrecking the transports' careful formation. The entire landings looked on the verge of collapse. Truscott boarded a launch in the dark and ferried himself one-by-one to all five assault transports, announcing H-Hour was delayed until 0430hrs. Several small French ships interposed themselves between the Allied transports and the beaches. Steamer *Lorraine* blinkered in French, "Be warned. Alert on shore for 0500." At 0430hrs, Truscott conferred with his staff, certain surprise had been lost.

Major Jon Dilley's 2nd BLT landed at Green Beach near the Sebou's mouth at 0540hrs and French defenders opened fire. Destroyer USS *Eberle* silenced the guns, but at 0630hrs French Dw.250s and LeO 451 bombers from Rabat-Salé began strafing US troops and warships. At 0700hrs, the Kasbah commenced firing at the US transports, which withdrew 15 miles, infuriating Truscott and crippling landing operations. By 0900hrs, 20 Wildcats from *Sangamon* and *Ranger* had driven off French aircraft, shooting down nine. Simultaneously, 2nd BLT captured the local lighthouse before being counterattacked hard by French infantry and 75mm artillery and driven back almost to the beaches.

French-speaking USAAF officers Colonel Demaw "Nick" Craw and Major Pierpont Hamilton had arrived ashore at daybreak on a daring diplomatic mission. Avoiding French strafing attacks and flying truce flags, they drove their jeep towards Port Lyautey. Upon approach, a nervous French machine gunner shot Craw dead. Port Lyautey's regretful Colonel Pétit arrested Hamilton and awaited the situation to clear.

Farthest south, Major Percy McCarley's 1st BLT was to land at beaches Yellow and Blue, but came ashore 2,800 yards north of Blue Beach, the second wave landing before the first at 0535hrs. Organizing themselves, 1st BLT rounded the lagoon to the south, then began advancing northeastwards. Strong French resistance pinned 1st BLT and was not overcome until dusk.

At 0630hrs, Lieutenant-Colonel John Toffey's 3rd BLT landed five miles north of their designated beaches, Red and Red 2, then were strafed by French fighters. By 0830hrs, 3rd BLT had shot down two Dewoitines and fought their way atop the 165ft coastal ridge. Slowly making order out of chaos, Toffey's 3rd BLT arrived at Hill 58 at midday and labored to organize follow-up waves at the beaches. Truscott, a veteran of the Dieppe disaster, came ashore that afternoon. No Goalpost D-Day objectives were met. Night fell with surf rising, all reserves committed, and the Americans' position precarious.

The battleship USS *Texas* (BB-35) at Virginia's Hampton Roads prior to *Torch*, August 19, 1942. Commissioned in 1914 and just missing an encounter with the High Seas Fleet on the morning of April 25, 1918, ancient sisters *Texas* and *New York* (BB-34) finally fired their guns in anger at Port Lyautey and Safi, respectively. (Navsource)

Gridlines are shown at intervals of 2km (1.24 miles)

US UNITS

1. USS *Dallas*

9th Infantry Division

2. 1st BLT, 60th Infantry Regiment
3. 2nd BLT, 60th Infantry Regiment
4. 3rd BLT, 60th Infantry Regiment
5. Company I, 3rd BLT
6. Companies K and M, 3rd BLT

2nd Armored Division

7. 1st Battalion, 66th Armored Regiment
8. Company C, 70th Tank Battalion

Goalpost
X X

TRUSCOTT

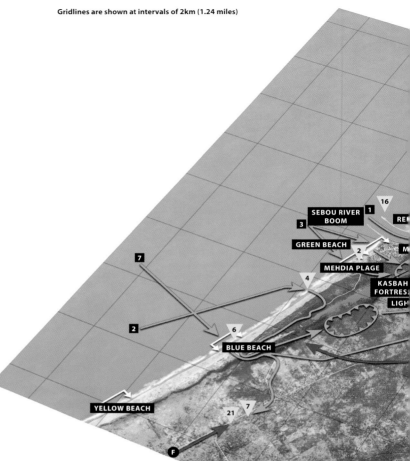

SEBOU RIVER BOOM `1`

`3`

GREEN BEACH `2`

MEHDIA PLAGE

`4`

KASBAH FORTRES...

LIGH...

`7`

`2`

`6`

BLUE BEACH

YELLOW BEACH

`21` `7`

F

`16`

RE...

EVENTS

November 8 (D-Day)

1. At dawn November 8, Colonel Craw and Major Hamilton drive a jeep under a flag of truce to parlay with French commander Colonel Petit. Just short of Port Lyautey, Colonel Craw is accidentally shot dead. Major Hamilton delivers his message to French HQ and is detained.

2. At 0540hrs, 2nd BLT begins landing at Green Beach and falls under French air and coastal artillery attack. Led by destroyer *Eberle*, all US ships are authorized to return fire at 0710hrs. 2nd BLT makes it ashore but inadvertently bypasses the Kasbah, reaching the lighthouse at 0900hrs and then to the Native Village.

3. At 1230hrs, I and II/1er RTM, supported by 75mm guns, counterattack 2nd BLT at Native Village, driving 2nd BLT back to the lighthouse by midnight.

4. 1st BLT lands in disarray at 0535hrs and at 1035hrs begins to advance towards Port Lyautey. 1st BLT is pinned by French machine-gun nests and the III/1er RTM advancing from Port Lyautey, but supporting artillery fire breaks up the French resistance at nightfall.

5. 3rd BLT inadvertently lands five miles too far north at 0630hrs and comes under French air attack. By 0830hrs, they summit the 165ft coastal ridge, but fail to advance on the airfield by the end of D-Day.

6. The 1st Armored Landing Team, 66th Armored Regiment, puts its first seven M5 Stuarts ashore at Blue Beach before nightfall.

November 9 (D+1)

7. Truscott expects a French counterattack from the south and sends all seven available M5 light tanks towards the highway at dawn. Shortly after 0600hrs, the US tanks repel a company of French infantry. Around 0640hrs, about 15 Renault FT-17s and two battalions of French infantry attack; the seven US tanks repulse them as well. Naval gunfire from *Savannah* wrecks the French assembly area in the woods.

8. Simultaneously, 1st BLT resumes advancing towards Port Lyautey airfield, but when cresting Mhignat Touama (Hill 52) is stopped by French mortar and heavy machine-gun fire. American artillery, naval fire, and ten recently arrived M5 Stuarts of Company C, 70th Tank Battalion spoil the impending French counterattack from the east. That afternoon, friendly fire disrupts plans to counterattack the French.

9. On the morning of D+1, the 3rd BLT's 105mm howitzers engage in an artillery duel with the French guns southwest of the airfield.

10. Overnight, the I/7e RTM had reinforced the Kasbah area. The following morning, D+1, the I/7e RTM attacks the disorganized 2nd BLT. American fire from the lighthouse temporarily drives the French out of Mehdia, but French reinforcements of 75mm guns and mortars evict the Americans from the lighthouse area. French 155mm fire from southwest of the airfield pins them down in the early afternoon. By nightfall, D+1 the Kasbah remains in French hands.

11. After dark, 3rd BLT's Company I crosses the Sebou but becomes disoriented and digs in on the southern bank.

November 10 (D+2)

12. US 3rd BLT's Companies K and M approach the western end of the Port Lyautey bridge in the early dark of November 10 and dislodge the French defenders before being repelled by French artillery. They leave a machine-gun platoon to block the bridge, then withdraw to Hill 58.

13. At 0100hrs, two hours after departing Mhignat Touama for the airfield, Company B of 1st BLT, inadvertently swinging to the east, is thwarted by a machine-gun outpost that disorganizes the unit. At daylight they are captured by troops of 7e RTM.

14. Elements of 1st BLT effect a set-piece attack on what they believe to be barracks, but is actually a café, capturing 75 civilians at 0430hrs. Nearby patrols capture another 100 French prisoners.

15. A joint demolition party sets out in a boat from transport *Clymer*, believes they have cut the Sebou River boom, and escapes under fire back to *Clymer* at 0430hrs.

16. Destroyer USS *Dallas*, carrying the raider detachment, enters the Sebou at 0530hrs and works her way upriver in the rain under heavy French fire from the Kasbah as *Kearny* takes out a French 75mm battery on cue. *Dallas* rams through the incompletely cut boom, then avoids the scuttled French ship *St Amiel* before running

FO... **MA...**

THE ASSAULT ON MEHDIA-PORT LYAUTEY, NOVEMBER 8–10, 1942

Hampered by difficult geography, resolute French resistance, and initially poor Army-Navy coordination, the Americans' Sub-Task Force Goalpost struggled to capture Mehdia-Port Lyautey. Improved combined-arms operations and green but resilient US infantry eventually overcame the stubborn French defense.

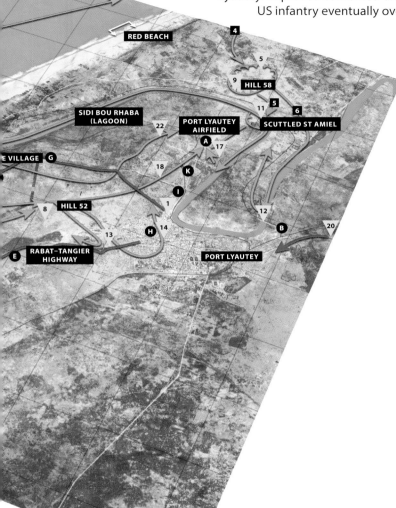

FRENCH UNITS
A. 128e DCA
B. 31e Génie (engineers)
Casablanca Division
C. I/1er RTM
D. II/1er RTM
E. III/1er RTM
F. Mechanized battalion, 1er RCA
Meknès Division
G. I/7e RTM
H. II/7e RTM
I. III/7e RTM
French batteries
J. Batterie Ponsot (two 138mm guns)
K. 1st Battery GPF (four 155mm guns)
L. The Kasbah:
7th rifle company, 1er RTM
Three FT-17 tanks
Défense des Passes (two 75mm guns on railcars)
1st Battery, 2e REI (four 75mm guns)
5th Battery, II/64e RAA (four 75mm guns)

PETIT

Meknès
DODY

aground near the airfield at 0737hrs. French artillery fire opens and is silenced by *Dallas*'s 3in. guns and US Navy seaplanes.

17. Debarking in rubber boats, the raiders assault the airfield from the east while Company I attacks from the north. The Americans secure the airfield by 0800hrs.

18. A 1st BLT company commander rallies 55 enlisted men. They advance at daybreak toward the airport, supported by recently arrived M5 tanks of Company C, 70th Tank Battalion. The M5s knock out four antitank guns and 28 machine guns, reaching the airfield at 1045hrs.

19. The 2nd BLT assaults the Kasbah and is repulsed by fierce French defensive fire.

Truscott calls in a Navy air strike. US infantry assaults and captures the Kasbah, taking 250 prisoners.

20. A truck column of French reinforcements approaches Port Lyautey from Meknès. Heavy 14in. fire from *Texas* wrecks it by 1131hrs.

21. Twenty FT-17 tanks counterattack from the south and are repulsed by US tanks, assault guns, and naval gunfire and air support.

22. The 2nd BLT, reinforced with an M7 Priest and an M5 Stuart, advances northeast with heavy fire support and ends the last French resistance near the airport at 1730hrs, taking 150 prisoners. The French open ceasefire negotiations at 2230hrs.

Truscott anticipated a French counterattack from the south and sent all seven available M5 Stuarts to block the Rabat highway. At 0600hrs, November 9, the Stuarts defeated an advancing company of French infantry, then at 0640hrs repulsed 15 Renault R35 tanks and two French infantry battalions, destroying four Renaults at no loss. Gunfire from *Savannah* wrecked the French assembly area in the woods nearby and the French withdrew. Meanwhile, 1st BLT marched northeast over wooded ridges towards Port Lyautey airfield seven miles distant but was delayed by heavy French resistance. French reinforcements at the Kasbah fought a back-and-forth battle with the 2nd BLT, finally driving the Americans from the lighthouse, then pinned down 2nd BLT with 155mm fire. Toffey's 3rd BLT dueled French artillery. That evening, Toffey dispatched three 3rd BLT companies on a nighttime end run against Port Lyautey's airfield and bridge. Throughout the night of November 9/10, 1st and 3rd BLTs closed on the airport and ancillary objectives. French defenders, American inexperience, and lingering disorganization from D-Day's chaotic landings continued to plague American operations.

Truscott dispatched his planned destroyer raid to the airport. Stripped-down and carrying 75 special assault troops, the old destroyer USS *Dallas* made for the Sebou mouth at 0400hrs, November 10, helmed by René Malvergne, Port Lyautey's Gaullist harbor pilot. Months earlier, a daring Office of Strategic Services (OSS) caper had spirited Malvergne to America. Now he returned. Fighting upriver through an ebb tide and torrential nighttime rain, *Dallas* ran aground and came under fire from the Kasbah. The fort's batteries straddled the destroyer several times while maximum revolutions struggled to power *Dallas* through the silt at a mere 2–3 knots. Drenched by near misses, *Dallas* suddenly broke free and rammed through the river boom at 18 knots, leaving the Kasbah astern.

As the destroyer surged upriver, more French batteries opened on her and were promptly shot out by *Dallas*'s 3in. guns; far offshore destroyer *Kearny*'s pre-arranged counter-battery fire eliminated another French 75mm. Now covered by *Savannah* floatplanes and increasingly cheered on by struggling American infantry, Malvergne swept *Dallas* past the scuttled *St Amiel* and around the last bend before running aground a final time. Full power again dragged *Dallas* through the mud until she pulled abeam the airfield at 0737hrs. Seventy-five raiders paddled to the airfield in rubber boats as *Dallas* traded fire with a final 75mm battery. A *Savannah* SOC Seagull silenced the offending guns with depth charges. The bold riverine charge had suffered zero casualties; a *Dallas* officer exclaimed, "The hand of God was right around us!" The raiders and 3rd BLT's Company I secured the airfield by 0800hrs. Battalion artillery and naval air and fire support neutralized French batteries nearby, while 3rd BLT secured Port Lyautey.

Pushing through heavy rain at dawn, 2nd BLT cleared French resistance outside the Kasbah walls by 0930hrs. As powerful US Navy units milled offshore without orders, four successive infantry assaults failed to take the Kasbah, driven back by withering rifle and machine-gun fire. Two M7 Priests fired 105mm rounds at point-blank range to no effect. Finally Truscott called in a Navy air

A 33rd Fighter Group P-40 launches from USS *Chenango* with catapult assistance, November 10, 1942. Of 77 P-40s, one crashed on take-off, one disappeared into the fog and was never seen again, and 17 were damaged on landing. None saw combat against the French. (NARA)

strike. Four Avengers and three Wildcats peeled off and showered the Kasbah with dozens of 100lb bombs. In a scene Truscott described as "a beautiful sight," and an after-action report "touches of *Beau Geste*," the Americans fixed bayonets, clutched grenades, and charged the Kasbah through the rainstorm yet again. This time the fortress fell, yielding 250 shell-shocked French prisoners. In assaulting the Kasbah that morning, the Americans had suffered 225 casualties.

Meanwhile strong French reinforcements approached Port Lyautey from Meknès. Battleship *Texas*, 17,000 yards out, hurled 214 14in. high-explosive rounds into the highway, achieving five direct hits. The devastated French convoy withdrew. With naval air and fire support, burgeoning US armor repulsed French armored counterattacks from Rabat.

Before sailing, the US Navy had requisitioned Standard Fruit Company's SS *Contessa* to ship 33rd Fighter Group's 1,000 tons of fuel and munitions. The banana freighter's crew had mutinied, forcing the Navy to raid Norfolk jails and press-gang convicts simply to get *Contessa* underway. Late on November 10, Malvergne successfully piloted the shabby, explosive-laden freighter nine miles up the Sebou to Port Lyautey's airfield. For his indispensable role in *Torch*, Malvergne was awarded the Silver Star. *Contessa*'s voyage proved Goalpost's last drama. At 2230hrs, November 10, the French expressed their desire for terms. Action at Mehdia-Port Lyautey ended at 0400hrs, November 11.

The battered front gate of Mehdia's Kasbah after the Port Lyautey battle. The romantic Truscott dreamed of bayonet charges and genuinely loved his infantry, but on November 10 he probably cost American lives by not earlier exploiting his idle naval firepower. (NARA)

The capture of Casablanca, November 9–11

Général Noguès had taken command of the French defense of Morocco and western Algeria and moved his headquarters to Fez. Noguès guarded inland routes and additionally rebuffed Luftwaffe requests to land at Moroccan airfields.

Delayed by the naval battle, Patton hadn't reached Fedala until 1320hrs on D-Day, his goal to "flay the idle, rebuke the incompetent, and drive the timid." Early on November 9, Patton investigated the logistical situation at the Fedala beaches, finding a leaderless mess and shore parties ducking for cover during French strafing attacks. Infuriated, Patton stalked the beaches all morning, personally sorting out supply foul-ups and inspiring listless personnel to perform their jobs with renewed vigor. Western Task Force headquarters set up in Fedala's Hotel Miramar, but communications with AFHQ would be plagued throughout the operation.

Meanwhile, French Hawk 75s, LeO 451s, and DB-7s harassed American infantry; VF-9 shot down four Hawk 75s, losing one Wildcat. At 1400hrs, an American air raid destroyed six Dw.250s, five Hawk 75s, and four DB-7s on the ground, ending French air resistance over Casablanca.

Task Force 34 suffered heavy landing craft attrition at Morocco, the result of high sea conditions, 14ft tides, and undertrained crews. Once stranded at low tide, the Atlantic surf easily wrecked the lightly built wooden vessels. Landing craft were never regarded as expendable; indeed the Western Allies endured strategy-affecting shortages through most of the war. (US Army)

The capture of Casablanca, November 8–11, 1942.

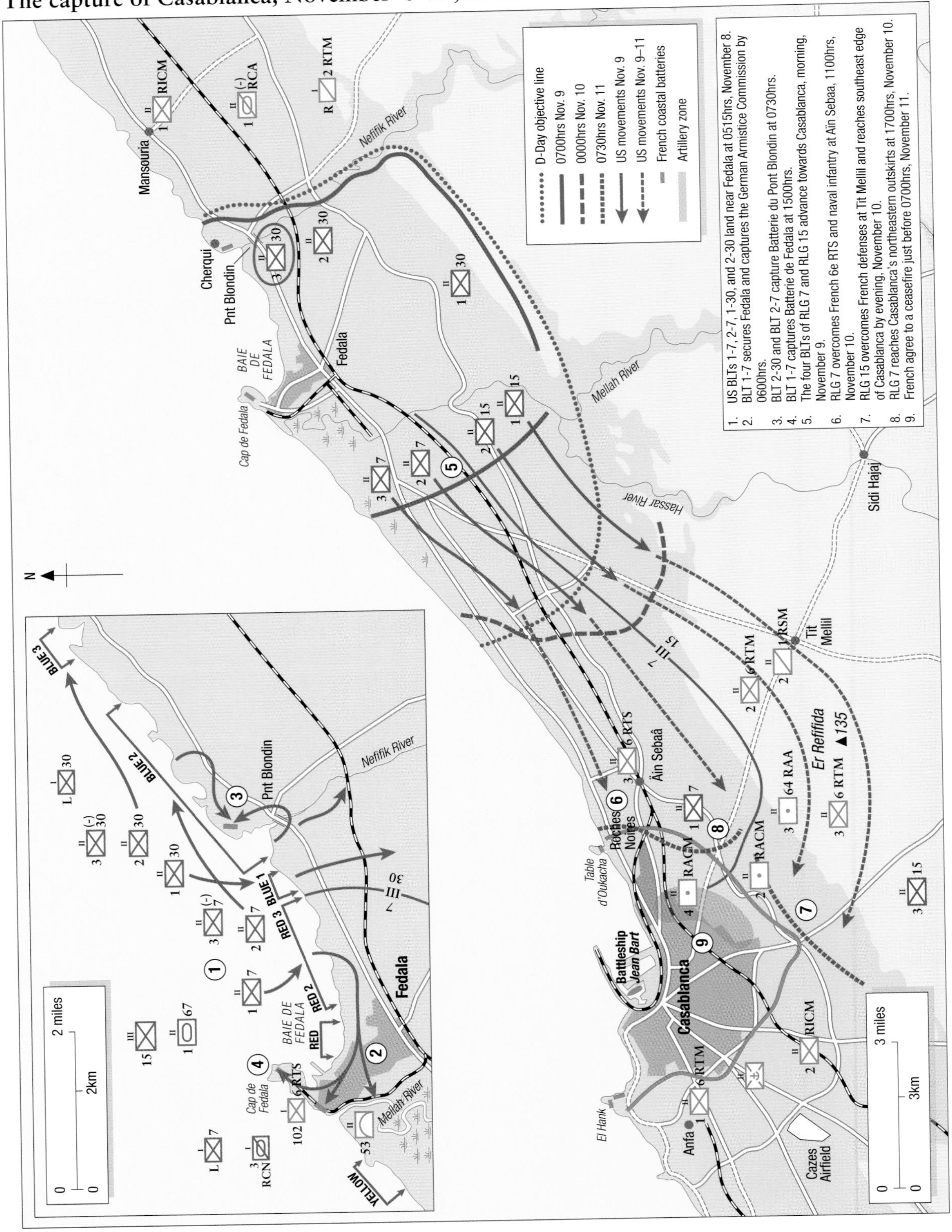

Legend:
- ······· D-Day objective line
- 0700hrs Nov. 9
- 0000hrs Nov. 10
- 0730hrs Nov. 11
- US movements Nov. 9
- US movements Nov. 9–11
- French coastal batteries
- Artillery zone

1. US BLTs 1-7, 2-7, 1-30, and 2-30 land near Fedala at 0515hrs, November 8. BLT 1-7 secures Fedala and captures the German Armistice Commission by 0600hrs.
2. BLT 2-30 and BLT 2-7 capture Batterie du Pont Blondin at 0730hrs.
3. BLT 1-7 captures Batterie de Fedala at 1500hrs.
4. The four BLTs of RLG 7 and RLG 15 advance towards Casablanca, morning, November 9.
5. RLG 7 overcomes French 6e RTS and naval infantry at Aïn Sebaa, 1100hrs, November 10.
6. RLG 15 overcomes French defenses at Tit Melili and reaches southeast edge of Casablanca by evening, November 10.
7. RLG 7 reaches Casablanca's northeastern outskirts at 1700hrs, November 10.
8. French agree to a ceasefire just before 0700hrs, November 11.

Map labels (main map):
- Mansouria
- Cherqui
- Pnt Blondin
- BAIE DE FEDALA
- Cap de Fedala
- Fedala
- Neflik River
- Melilh River
- Hassar River
- Sidi Hajaï
- Tit Melili
- Er Reffida ▲135
- Aïn Sebaà
- Roches Noires
- Table d'Oukacha
- Casablanca
- Battleship Jean Bart
- Anfa
- El Hank
- Cazes Airfield

Units: 1 RICM, 1 (-) RCA, R 2 RTM, 31-30, 2-30, 1-30, 1-15, 2-7, 3-7, 2-RSM, 2 6 RTM, 2 RACM, 64 RAA, 3 6 RTM, 3 6 RTS, 1 7, 4 RACM, 1 6 RTM, 2 RICM, 3-15

Inset map labels:
- Pnt Blondin
- Neflik River
- BLUE 3
- BLUE 2
- BLUE 1
- RED 3
- RED 2
- RED
- Fedala
- BAIE DE FEDALA
- Melilh River
- Cap de Fedala
- YELLOW

Inset units: L 30, 3 (-) 30, 2 30, 1 30, III 7, 1 (-) 7, 2 7, 1 7, 1 67, 15, L 7, 3 RCN, 102 6 RTS, 53

Scales: 2 miles / 2km; 3 miles / 3km

N

Under Major-General Jonathan Anderson, Sub-Task Force Brushwood advanced southwesterly from Fedala towards Casablanca on a four-battalion front. Along the coast were BLT 3-7 and BLT 2-7 of RLG 7. Inland was RLG 15, composed of BLT 2-15 and BLT 1-15. Initial French resistance was light: strafing by occasional aircraft, a morning reconnaissance patrol driven off, and 30 vehicles at the Fedala–Boulhat intersection repulsed by naval air support. Brushwood's greatest enemy was logistics. By 1700hrs, November 9, US transports had unloaded 55 percent of personnel, 31 percent of vehicles, and just 3 percent of supplies.

French battleship *Jean Bart* at her Casablanca pier, November 1942. The dramatic stern damage is the result of a 1,000lb bomb delivered via a *Ranger* Dauntless on November 10. *Jean Bart* eventually settled the remaining few feet to rest on the shallow harbor bottom. (Navsource)

As Brushwood closed on Casablanca on November 10, French resistance stiffened. Rescued sailors reinforced French infantry and artillery, while two French corvettes braved sorties to shell RLG 7, advancing against strong 75mm and 90mm fire. As cruiser *Augusta* chased the corvettes, she was straddled by the suddenly operational *Jean Bart*. Nine Ranger Dauntlesses retaliated and at 1600hrs, two 1,000lb bombs dismissed *Jean Bart* from the battle for good. Meanwhile, French submarines *Tonnant*, *Meduse*, and *Antiope* attacked US carrier *Ranger*, battleship *Massachusetts*, and cruiser *Tuscaloosa*. All torpedoes missed.

East of Casablanca at Aïn Sebaa, fierce French resistance from 6e RTM, naval infantry, and 90mm AA guns delayed US infantry and M5 Stuarts. Two French naval platoons were encircled and suffered 50 percent casualties before surrendering. Eventually, heavy US naval fire compelled a French withdrawal at 1100hrs. RLG 15 overcame strong organized defense inland at the village of Tit Mellil and reached the southeastern edge of Casablanca by evening. RLG 7 reached Casablanca's northern outskirts at 1700hrs. Brushwood's casualties for the day came to 36 dead and 113 wounded.

At Gibraltar, AFHQ grew worried at Patton's lack of communication, not realizing it was a technical issue. The afternoon of November 10, Eisenhower got a message through to Patton: "Dear George: Only tough nut left to crack is in your hands. Crack it open quickly. Ike." Angrily feeling second-guessed, Patton prepared to "bombard hell" out of Casablanca the following morning. Recently arrived battleship *New York* reinforced cruisers *Augusta* and *Cleveland* to provide naval gunfire support. Harmon's Shermans from Safi had not yet arrived, while Port Lyautey's airstrip proved too damaged for 33rd Fighter Group operations.

An M5 Stuart light tank of the US 70th Tank Battalion at Casablanca, November 17, 1942. Modifications from the original M3 included twin Cadillac V8s, automatic Hydra-Matic transmissions, and sloped glacis armor, but the M5 retained its predecessor's underpowered 37mm gun. (NARA)

Defending Casablanca were 3,600 French infantry, 90 guns, and cannibalized naval units. Late on November 10, Darlan ordered Noguès to terminate hostilities; the ceasefire was agreed only minutes before Patton's planned bombardment at 0700hrs, November 11 – coincidentally Armistice Day and Patton's 57th birthday. Patton, an ardent Francophile, conducted a gracious armistice at Fedala that afternoon. Altogether Western Task Force had suffered 459 killed and missing, 637 wounded, and 71 captured.

All three Allied invasions had been successful. The French had never been capable of prolonged military resistance against concentrated Allied strength, and

the chaotic political situation had further exasperated coordinated defense. Inexplicably, *Torch*'s November 8–10 combat is too often dismissed as a historical footnote. Yet in three days defending North Africa against the Anglo-Americans, the French had suffered 3,343 casualties, including 1,346 killed. When including French- and Axis-inflicted naval losses, total Allied combat casualties climb to 2,661, including 1,331 killed or missing – fully 30 percent that suffered by the lionized June 6, 1944 Normandy landings.

POST-INVASION BEDLAM

The *Torch* landings stunned the Axis, who immediately expected full French collaboration to repel the Allies. With metropolitan France practically hostage, the Axis demanded unconditional access to Tunisian airdromes on November 9. By noon, the first in an eventual flood of Luftwaffe transports began landing at El Aouina near Tunis. French soldiers surrounded the airfield but did nothing as ever more German paratroopers arrived; they were joined that afternoon by 27 Luftwaffe fighters and 24 Stukas. II Fliegerkorps commander General der Flieger Bruno Loerzer brazenly drove through the airfield cordon to personally obtain a Tunisia-wide guarantee of French non-resistance from Vice-Amiral Jean-Pierre Estéva, Tunisia's Resident-General. In Munich, Hitler summoned the Vichy delegation, now increasingly aware of their nation's menacing new predicament. Initially, Hitler praised the "loyal" French for fighting the Allies, but his mood darkened by the hour. Separately, Hitler schemed with Mussolini's foreign minister Count Ciano to buy time until *Case Anton* was ready.

That day, Giraud appeared in Algiers where a freed Robert Murphy awkwardly explained that Darlan was now part of the political equation. *Torch* deputy Clark met the top French leaders at Algiers' St George Hotel and discovered they categorically rejected Giraud, considering him a traitor. The entire Giraud scheme had proved a total fiasco; indeed, Mast was in hiding and Béthouart awaiting execution. The following morning, Darlan agreed to order a ceasefire without Pétain's express permission. That afternoon, Pétain, under duress, officially fired Darlan, who then frantically tried to rescind the ceasefire before Clark arrested him. Pétain then secretly messaged the Allies that he approved.

As November 10 expired, so too did all Nazi pretense of friendly cooperation with Vichy France. At midnight, the panzers, stayed since June 1940, began to roll again. Ten Wehrmacht divisions surged into unoccupied France, racing uncontested towards the sea. From southwest France General Johannes Blaskowitz's 1.Armee advanced parallel to the Pyrenees while Generaloberst Friedrich Dollmann's 7.Armee drove south from central France. By evening November 11, German forces had reached the Mediterranean. Simultaneously, six Italian divisions occupied southeastern France and Corsica. *Case Anton*'s only blemish occurred at Toulon, home of the Marine Nationale. Fearing French sabotage, Wehrmacht officers lost their nerve, halted short of the port, and opened negotiations. The tense standoff would climax November 27 as panzers suddenly surged into Toulon – Operation *Lila*. With minutes to spare, alert French sailors mass scuttled virtually the entire French fleet, infuriating their German occupiers.

Despite *Lila*'s failure, all metropolitan France was now immersed beneath the Wehrmacht. The Vichy state was fully revealed as the political fraud it had always been.

Just when Rommel predicted El Alamein had doomed the Axis armies to destruction in North Africa, Hitler suddenly declared North Africa vital and doubled down on the theater. Supplies and reinforcements Rommel had so badly needed now poured into Tunisia. The Allies had predicted this reaction, but not its sheer efficiency. The Wehrmacht's response was what it did so well: urgent improvisation. A furious Luftwaffe airbridge transferred infantry and fighter squadrons to Tunisian airfields, while slower merchantmen shipped Axis heavy weapons to the ports at Bizerte and Tunis, 40 miles apart. Ground units would buy time with an "inkblot" strategy, consolidating and expanding the twin Tunisian bridgeheads. Axis offensive action would be limited to spoiling attacks to keep the Allies out of the vital ports while sufficient strength accumulated.

Tunisia's Dorsal Mountains run north to south, geographically dividing the region. Axis airfields on the eastern slopes lay in the mountains' rain shadow, giving the Axis clear skies when Allied aircraft to the west would be grounded by weather. From the mountains' divide, rivers cut passes as they flow west to east towards the Gulf of Tunis. The major roads and railways to Bizerte and Tunis naturally followed the river valleys, providing the Axis predictable choke points. An Allied officer called Tunisia "a country of defiles" while an American major noted the front was "about fifty feet wide – just across the road and a little to either side of it." Road and rail networks converged at Mateur, 22 miles from Bizerte, and at Djedeïda, 13 miles from Tunis, obvious midway objectives. Most of Tunisia's annual 25in. of rain falls in the winter between November and February, turning the semi-arid landscape into impassable mud.

Amphibious invasions have been defined as a race to see which side can most quickly build up decisive reinforcements. The last two months of 1942 would see this truism played out over half of North Africa's coastline: the "Race for Tunis." Allied front-line ground strength would be weak and air support insufficient. Though grossly outnumbered, geography, weather, and logistics favored the Axis' Tunisian defense.

The Allies' ultimate objectives were Tunisia's two major ports: Bizerte and Tunis. The seizure of both would immediately doom the Axis in Tunisia and by extension North Africa. Logistics were crucial. From Casablanca to Tunis ran a 1,410-mile, single-track, standard-gauge railway with a daily one-way capacity of 12 trains and 2,880 tons. In Tunisia, narrower meter-gauge lines branched to the ports of Bougie, Philippeville, and Bône. Frail, dilapidated French locomotives and rolling stock were powered by scarce imported coal. Two main roads connected Algiers to northern Tunisia: a narrow coastal road via Bougie, Philippeville, and Bône, and a wider road farther inland that followed the railway. Altogether

German troops obliviously inspect their PzKpfw IV while the scuttled French cruiser *Colbert* blazes at its Toulon berth, November 27, 1942. A grimly vindicated Darlan wrote to Churchill: "I told you we would never surrender the fleet. It seems you didn't believe me." (Bundesarchiv, Bild 101I-027-1451-10/Vennemann, Wolfgang/CC-BY-SA 3.0)

A Moroccan labor gang at Casablanca, November 1942. The chaotic supply situation on North African beaches required the natives' cheap, raw manpower. Arab laborers were paid daily with cigarettes, food, and cloth, finding weekly salaries incomprehensible. Within days at Safi, tons of pilfered American food and ammunition were found stashed on local Arab fishing boats. (US Army)

the transportation network was wholly inadequate for a modern army and would be increasingly strained as the Allies advanced, yet Axis forces were just 100 miles from their logistic base in Sicily.

Since 1940, Tunisia's French garrison had been upgraded to 15,000 troops, 20 armored cars, and some antiaircraft units. The French found themselves in an impossible situation. Two far superior, mutually hostile armies converged remorselessly on Tunisia, while conflicting, incomprehensible orders emanated from both Vichy and Algiers. Neither Axis nor Allies held any regard for the Tunisian government's feeble assertions of neutrality.

On November 11, the Heer's Colonel Hans Lederer appeared in Tunis to take command of German ground forces. The following day came three companies of paratroopers and panzergrenadiers. The French had blocked the Tunisian ports, but Italian engineers quickly cleared the harbors and the first two Italian transports docked in Bizerte, unloading 340 troops, 17 tanks, four guns, 55 trucks, 40 tons of ammunition, and 101 tons of fuel.

The Italian Superga division under Generale di Divisione Dante Lorenzelli began to arrive in Tunisia November 12, followed by the German 11.Fallschirmjäger-Pionier-Bataillon, a reconnaissance company, motorcycles, and a panzer company. Within days, 67 Bf 109s, 14 Fw 190s, and 28 Ju 87 Stukas had transferred to Tunisia while Bizerte alone was averaging 50 Ju 52 landings a day.

Caught flatfooted on D-Day, the Luftwaffe and Kriegsmarine had begun to strike the *Torch* convoys with a vengeance. Off Algiers, the disabled *Leedstown* was hit by two torpedoes at 1310hrs, November 9 and abandoned. She sank at 1615hrs. The next day, *U-431* torpedoed and sank destroyer HMS *Martin*, killing 127, while Italian torpedo bombers sank sloop HMS *Ibis*, 10 miles north of Algiers, killing another 117. On November 11, over 50 Axis bombers managed a single bomb hit on escort carrier HMS *Argus*, killing four, while off Casablanca *U-173* torpedoed transport *Joseph Hewes*, tanker *Winooski*, and destroyer *Hambleton* within eight minutes, sinking *Joseph Hewes* and killing two dozen sailors. The following day, *U-130* torpedoed and sank transports *Edward Rutledge*, *Tasker H. Bliss*, and *Hugh L. Scott*, killing 108.

U-boats then mauled an Atlantic-bound *Torch* return convoy early on November 15. *U-155* torpedoed escort carrier HMS *Avenger*; she sank in minutes, taking 516 of her 528 men with her. *Ettrick* was hit and eventually sank, while *Almaack* was torpedoed but towed successfully to Gibraltar. That same day, *U-173* struck cargo ship USS *Electra* 17 miles off Fedala; *Electra* miraculously survived. The following day, destroyers USS *Swanson* and USS *Quick* cornered *U-173* off Casablanca and depth-charged her into oblivion.

A few days earlier on November 13, Clark and Murphy had hammered out a temporary collaboration plan with the French; Pétain's secret approval had broken the deadlock. French North Africa had officially thrown its lot in with the Allies and would fight the Axis. Darlan declared himself French North Africa's High Commissioner and named Giraud commander-in-chief of French land and air forces.

The slapdash arrangement was a true "shotgun wedding." De Gaulle and his supporters – with their unassailable moral record – were outraged at being shut out of power in favor of former Nazi collaborators. The formal Clark–Darlan Agreement of November 22 detailed and codified political, economic, and military matters. The Americans secured categorical pardon of all French officers who had revolted against Vichy. That day, French West Africa also announced it would abandon Vichy and join the Allies.

The deal was a shock to the high-minded American and British publics. The nations' media reacted virulently to the "Darlan Deal;" one newspaper described it as "getting in bed with the arch Nazi collaborationist." Under fire, Roosevelt eventually admitted it was "a temporary expedient" and quoted what he claimed to remember as an old Romanian proverb: "My friends, I am told that in times of grave danger it is permissible to hold the hand of the devil until you have crossed the bridge." Darlan himself sensed his utility, telling Clark, "I am to be used and thrown away." Roosevelt was too politically savvy to hand-wring over a deal that could shorten the war and wired Eisenhower his full backing of the decision. US ambassador to Britain Gil Winant stated bluntly, "It means the saving of infinite time and 50,000 American lives … It was worth it."

Brokering the "Darlan Deal" was a major Allied victory. Without French help, occupying and administering North Africa would have been a nightmare and absorbed troops available for combat. Eisenhower reported, "It is impossible to exaggerate the degree to which, in carrying on the fight in Tunisia, we are dependent upon the good will and cooperation of the French."

The Americans agreed to supply and begin rearming the poorly equipped Armée d'Afrique. Giraud named Juin Algerian field commander. Général de corps Louis-Marie Koeltz's XIXe Région Militaire would be the main French formation on the front, operating independently on the Allies' right in the south. Meanwhile, Giraud continued to suggest he should be Allied commander-in-chief.

The Gulf of Tunis viewed from Carthage. This 1943 oil painting by Henry Carr was a commission of the War Artists Advisory Committee. The lifeblood of Axis forces in North Africa flowed through this Gulf, particularly after Montgomery's Eighth Army seized Rommel's Libyan ports. (IWM LD 3230)

First Allied drive on Tunis, November 25–30, 1942.

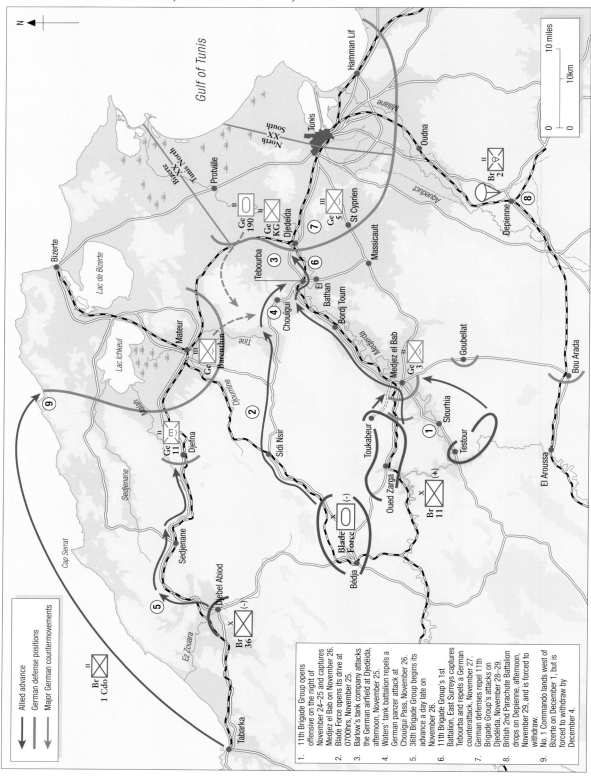

Legend (lower left):
- Allied advance
- German defense positions
- Major German countermovements

1. 11th Brigade Group opens offensive on the night of November 24–25 and captures Medjez el Bab on November 26. Blade Force opens its drive at 0700hrs, November 25.
2. Barlow's tank company attacks the German airfield at Djedeïda, afternoon, November 25.
3. Waters' tank battalion repels a German panzer attack at Chouïgui Pass, November 26. 36th Brigade Group begins its advance a day late on November 26.
4. 11th Brigade Group's 1st Battalion, East Surreys captures Tebourba and repels a German counterattack, November 27.
5. German defenses repel 11th Brigade Group's attacks on Djedeïda, November 28–29.
6. British 2nd Parachute Battalion drops on Depienne, afternoon, November 29, and is forced to withdraw.
7. No. 1 Commando lands west of Bizerte on December 1, but is forced to withdraw by December 4.

Axis forces in Tunisia were vulnerable but strengthening by the hour. The Germans sufficiently bullied temporarily superior French forces into allowing the frenetic Axis build-up while avoiding prematurely provoking the French into hostilities. Wily French Général de division Georges Barré sought to stall the Axis as long as possible while quietly withdrawing towards Allied lines and preparing his Tunis Division for imminent combat.

THE RACE FOR TUNIS

On November 9, British Lieutenant-General Kenneth Anderson had arrived at the transport *Bulolo* and taken command of Eastern Task Force as planned. Moving east, Anderson would capture coastal airfields for friendly air support, then successively seize the ports of Bougie, Philippeville, and Bône via amphibious leaps, troop-lifting C-47s, and "every kind of scrawny vehicle that can run." AFHQ would send reinforcements as urgently as primitive North African communications allowed. Dominating all AFHQ concerns was the knowledge that maybe three weeks of tolerable weather remained before the arrival of Tunisia's winter downpours. The window to seize Tunis and Bizerte before the undeveloped country became an impassable quagmire was therefore small indeed.

AFHQ redesignated Eastern Task Force "British First Army," but "Army" reflected future plans. Currently, First Army comprised only Major-General Vyvyan Evelegh's British 78th Infantry Division, itself comprising 11th Brigade Group and 36th Brigade Group. Anderson's third formation was the provisional Blade Force, consisting of 2,500 British and American troops, 36 Valentine tanks, 24 Crusader IIIs, and 54 US M3 Stuarts, as well as 25-pdr field guns and 6-pdr antitank guns. US Army units in Oran and Morocco would trickle piecemeal to First Army as urgently as possible, while British 6th Armoured Division would arrive within weeks. Mixing national formations was inefficient but unavoidable. As reinforcements arrived, Eisenhower expected to eventually field two separate British and American corps.

Eastern Task Force's floating reserve, 36th Brigade Group, set out by sea and occupied Bougie on November 11. The following day 36th BG occupied Djidjelli, but back at Bougie Axis aircraft bombed and sank transports *Karanja*, *Cathay*, and *Awatea* and heavily damaged monitor Roberts, while antiaircraft auxiliary *Tynwald* was sunk by torpedo. Meanwhile, two companies of 3rd Parachute Battalion airdropped to occupy Bône and No. 6 Commando landed by sea to occupy the port. A day later, November 13, the main body of 36th Brigade Group departed Bougie, one battalion by rail to Sétif and another battalion by sea to Bône. The 36th Brigade Group was joined in Bône November 15 by the 150-man Hart Force, a provisional reconnaissance unit. That same day, 36th Brigade Group's advance elements occupied Tabarka while 33 C-47s dropped 350 paratroopers of Lieutenant-Colonel Raff's *Villain*-decimated 2nd/509th

An Allied freighter unloads a US Army CCKW-352 2½-ton truck on the dock at Algiers. Lack of convoy shipping space greatly cut into motor transport. The Allies requisitioned local vehicles, including 380 charcoal-burning trucks from an Oran wine company. Nevertheless, Allied motorized transport was in very short supply during the Race for Tunis. (IWM A 12826)

PIR on Youks-les-Bains' airfield. Raff then secured Tébessa airfield ten miles east before marching 80 miles southeast into Tunisia. US 64th Troop Carrier Group dropped 384 troops of 1st Parachute Battalion at Souk el Arba November 16, while vanguard 36th Brigade Group units reached Djebel Abiod, both making contact with Barré's French.

Afrika Korps commander General der Panzertruppen Walther Nehring had been convalescing in Berlin since August. En route back to Egypt, he was suddenly transferred to Tunisia to take command of XC Korps. Nehring arrived November 17 and chose to aggressively extend the Bizerte and Tunis bridgeheads. That day, at 1430hrs, advancing German–Italian armored reconnaissance engaged British troops at Djebel Abiod – *Torch*'s first ground combat between Axis and Allies. After three hours, the Germans and Italians withdrew, losing eight tanks, one killed, and 20 wounded. The British also suffered casualties and lost significant guns and vehicles. The 78th Division established its headquarters at Bône, and Hart Force had advanced east of Djebel Abiod.

German PzKpfw III Ausf. N medium tanks unloading at Bizerte, late November or December 1942. AFHQ grumbled at the French vigorously resisting the Allies for three days but meekly acquiescing to the Axis counter-invasion. This was grossly unfair criticism: French officers were painfully aware their homes and families in metropolitan France were potential hostages to Nazi Germany. (*Signal* magazine)

Small elements of Anderson's Blade Force reinforced Barré's French troops at Medjez el Bab the afternoon of November 18. Early the next morning, Barré received an ultimatum from Nehring. Shortly afterwards, at 0915hrs, the Germans opened fire. The Allies and French repulsed several infantry attacks, but German combined-arms assaults and Stuka dive-bombing eventually compelled them to retreat; First Army was strictly conserving its strength for a major offensive and not inclined to piecemeal reinforcements. The Allies withdrew from Medjez el Bab early on November 20.

An M3 Lee medium tank and crew at Souk el Arba, Tunisia, November 23, 1942. The M3 was a stopgap imposed by the 1941 American steel industry's turret-casting limitations. The tank's towering profile inspired a crewman's well-documented remark, "It looks like a damned cathedral coming down the road." (US Army Signal Corps)

Meanwhile at Bédja, First Army marshalled for its main offensive, but the area was repeatedly hammered by the Luftwaffe, beginning most heavily on November 20. Thirty Ju 87s and Ju 88s bombed Maison Blanche, destroying ten Allied aircraft and expelling the forward-based B-17s to muddy, unsurfaced "Tafaraoui deep and gooey." American heavy bombers now faced 1,200-mile round trips to Bizerte and Tunis. By November 24, the Bizerte and Tunis bridgeheads had merged and Nehring prepared for the expected Allied offensive. Generalmajor Wolfgang Fischer arrived to command 10.Panzer-Division and on November 25, Eisenhower transferred AFHQ from Gibraltar to Algiers.

First Army attacks, November 25

Geography for First Army's east–northeast advance on Bizerte and Tunis dictated three parallel axes of advance: 36th Brigade Group in the north from Djebel Abiod towards Bizerte; Blade Force in the center from Bédja towards Tunis; and 11th Brigade Group in the south from Oued Zarga and Testour. Various American units were attached to each formation. Facing Anderson in Tunisia were 15,575 German and 9,000 Italian troops, including part of the Superga Division and advance elements of XXX Corpo.

In the south, 11th Brigade Group opened the Allied offensive, pushing towards Medjez el Bab the night of November 24/25. A reinforced infantry battalion was to strike from each flank, with a third element to seize high ground nearby as a reserve. Defending Medjez el Bab were five companies of Germans and Italians. The 11th Brigade Group's northernmost unit, the 2nd Battalion, Lancashire Fusiliers, attacked over open ground in brilliant moonlight. German machine-gun fire erupted, cutting down the 2nd/Lancashires' commander. The Lancashires took cover and as day arrived were further pinned down by German artillery. That afternoon, the Germans counterattacked with panzers and infantry in the face of British artillery fire and the British withdrawal approached a rout. From the south–southwest, 5th Battalion, Northamptonshires, reinforced by US artillery, briefly claimed 250m Djebel Bou Mouss, but were shortly driven off by panzers from Medjez el Bab. However, that night the Germans stealthily withdrew and the following day, 11th Brigade Group attacked and captured a mostly empty Medjez el Bab.

The 11th Brigade Group advanced against stiffer German resistance, but the Germans withdrew again, this time to Djedeïda. In the early dark of November 27, 1st Battalion, East Surreys captured Tebourba, a town of about 4,000. Later that morning, German armor sharply counterattacked and a nasty day-long melée developed in the surrounding olive groves. At dusk, the panzers retired towards Djedëida, leaving severe damage behind them.

In the center, Blade Force's 104 Allied tanks had opened their drive at 0700hrs, November 25, defeating light resistance from German–Italian patrols. After crossing the Tine River, Blade Force commander Colonel R. A. Hull ordered Lieutenant-Colonel Waters' US 1st Battalion, 1st Armored Regiment to create a "tank-infested area" southeast of Mateur and scout crossings of the Medjerda River for 11th Brigade Group's later use. As Waters' battalion approached Chouïgui Pass, a company of the 11.Fallschirmjäger-Pionier-Bataillon, reinforced by Italian antitank guns, conducted a skillful defense that frustrated American and British efforts all day before retiring that night.

Meanwhile, M3 Stuarts of Major Rudolph Barlow's Company C had broken out of Chouïgui Pass and destroyed an unsuspecting German sentry position before being bombed and strafed by German aircraft. Dutifully continuing on their river scouting mission, they stumbled upon a brand-new, undefended Luftwaffe base at the Djedëida airstrip. Overcoming their shock, Barlow's 17 M3 Stuart light tanks rampaged through the hapless airdrome, destroying 24 Bf 109s and Ju 87s before withdrawing. The fantastic episode inspired near panic at German headquarters, as Nehring believed major Allied forces were just five miles from Tunis. Kesselring toured the Tunisian bridgehead and assured Nehring it was an isolated incident, correctly believing that the Allied offensive would continue to be methodical and cautious.

The following day, November 26, the Germans dispatched a battalion-sized task force south towards Waters' battalion at Chouïgui Pass; the German formation comprised six 75mm-gunned PzKpfw IVs and three 50mm-gunned PzKpfw IIIs. With few options available, Waters' outgunned Stuarts desperately ambushed the panzers. Major Carl Siglin's Company A dangerously lured German fire while Company B attacked the panzers' flanks and rear at such close range the M3s' 37mm "squirrel guns" were effective.

Participating at the battle for "Happy Valley," Lieutenant Freeland Daubin, Jr later offered the following grim, sardonic account of his Stuart crew's ordeal (abridged here for space):

A heavy barrage of Allied antiaircraft fire streaks skyward during a night-time Axis air raid on Maison Blanche Airfield, November 21, 1942. On November 27, the first night-equipped Beaufighters arrived in Algiers and immediately shot down three Luftwaffe bombers. (IWM NA 000176)

The 37mm of the little American M3 light tank popped and spat like an angry cap pistol [at] the Mark IV. The Jerry seemed annoyed by these attentions. Questing about with his incredibly long, bell-snouted, "souped-up" 75mm KwK 40 rifle, the German soon spotted his heckler. Deciding to do the sporting thing and lessen the extreme range, he leisurely commenced closing the 140-yard gap between himself and the light tank. In a frenzy of desperation and fading faith in their highly touted weapon, the M3 crew pumped more than 18 rounds at the Jerry tank while it came in. Through the scope sight, the tracer could be seen to hit, then glance straight up.

The M3 commander decided he was in a situation known in the trade as "situation doubtful." The feeling as the M3 lurched backward up the wadi bank was one of relief – no one enjoys playing "clay pigeon M3." Death, unexpectedly deferred these many seconds, struck as the light tank bounced out of the wadi. The slug struck the vertical surface of the heavy armored driver's door and literally caved in the front of the M3. With its driver instantly dead, the bow gunner blind, stunned and bleeding, the loader cut down by machine-gun fire as he sought cover, and its commander lying wounded on the ground, the little tank, though sheathed in flame, backed on through the battle until stopped by friendly hands.

The Americans lost six Stuarts and several men, including Siglin, but destroyed all six PzKpfw IVs and a PzKpfw III. The US Army had won its first-ever tank battle against the Wehrmacht. As the Germans withdrew, British artillery and the 17th/21st Lancers knocked out another PzKpfw III, while 1st Parachute Battalion occupied the evacuated ground. But Allied failure to more boldly exploit the recent unexpected tactical victories rendered them strategically meaningless.

Farthest north, 36th Brigade Group hadn't made the schedule and didn't advance until November 26, finding the Germans had withdrawn. Further caution compounded the original delay, and already 36th Brigade Group had become irrelevant to the offensive. The Luftwaffe asserted its air superiority, hampering Allied movement. Eleven inexperienced P-38s repulsed German bombers, then inexplicably strafed a company of the US 701st Tank Destroyer Battalion in a sustained friendly fire incident, killing five, wounding 16, and damaging most vehicles and guns. By November 27, the Allied drive was clearly stalling. Evelegh adjusted, planning a new attack, to be assisted behind the lines by a 2nd Parachute Battalion airdrop and an amphibious landing by No. 1 Commando. Axis reinforcements continued to arrive, including Generalmajor Fischer's 10.Panzer-Division.

Evelegh's altered attack commenced badly on November 28 as his troops encountered their first PzKpfw VI Tiger tanks and MG 42 machine guns. On the coast west of Djefna, the Germans ambushed elements of the Argyll and Sutherland Highlanders, destroying ten Bren Gun Carriers and inflicting 116 killed and captured. The 11th Brigade Group launched the main attack against Djedëida at 1300hrs, led by a battalion each from the Northamptonshires and the US 12th Armored Regiment. Eben Emael veteran Major Rudolf Witzig's excellently prepared defenses repulsed 11th Brigade Group, destroying five M3 Lees. A self-satisfied German report proclaimed "a Tunisian Verdun on a minor scale."

The following morning, November 29, the reinforced 11th Brigade Group attacked again. Forced to advance through open ground, 11th Brigade Group was savaged by Stukas. Enduring the relentless dive-bombing, a British Army captain conceded, "Like all things German, it is very efficient and goes on much too long." Unknown to either side, *Torch* had reached its high water mark; Tunis' minarets were faintly visible from Djedëida, "to remain a haunting memory through many tough days ahead," recollected a US tank commander. The Allies would not again come so close to Tunis until May 1943.

German air superiority was the decisive factor. Evelegh recommended suspending the attack until December 2, when a forward Allied airfield at Medjez el Bab was expected to be operational. AFHQ approved. That afternoon, 44 C-47s dropped 2nd Parachute Battalion's 530 paratroopers on Depienne, 25 miles from Tunis. Discovering their objective Oudna airfield unoccupied and the Tunis

A 1943 oil painting by Henry Carr depicts a camouflaged British 25-pdr gun in action near Medjez el Bab. Despite logistical difficulties, the Allies employed field artillery at the front in greater numbers than the Axis. However, this advantage would eventually be negated by German air superiority and the immobilizing winter rains. (IWM LD 3231)

Three British officers of the decimated 2nd Parachute Battalion resting at Bédja, a fortnight after the disastrous Depienne drop, mid-December 1942. Coastal Tunisia's grassy hills and gray winter overcast are readily apparent in this photo. (IWM NA 351)

MAJOR RUDOLPH BARLOW'S COMPANY C, 1ST ARMORED REGIMENT, DJEDEÏDA, NOVEMBER 25, 1942 (PP. 78–79)

Scouting Medjerda River crossings near Djedeïda on November 25, 1942, the 17 M3 Stuart light tanks of Major Rudolph Barlow's Company C, 1st Armored Regiment pulled behind a low ridge and observed a brand-new Luftwaffe airfield bustling with Bf 109Gs of JG 53 and Ju 87D Stukas of StG 3. Bewildered, Barlow radioed battalion commander Lieutenant-Colonel John Waters: "Right in front of me is an airport full of German airplanes, sitting there, the men all sitting out on gasoline barrels, shooting the breeze in the sunlight. What should I do?" Waters' response: "For God's sakes attack them! Go after them!"

"At this point," records the official US Army history, "one of the most bizarre incidents of World War II ensued." All 17 Stuarts (**1**) surged over the ridge onto the airstrip where the German aircraft were packed like "fat geese on a small pond." Germans waved, assuming the tanks were Italian. Then Barlow's tanks unleashed their wild mêlée, dispersing over the airfield with abandon, firing 37mm guns and machine guns, shooting up supporting buildings, igniting fuel barrels, and crushing aircraft and personnel beneath their tank treads. Luftwaffe crew fled for any available cover or escape. One Stuart drove straight down a

line of parked planes, methodically shearing off their tails one after another.

A German flyer referred to a "mad scramble" as aircraft tried to escape by taking off in any possible direction. A second German reported missing a head-on collision with another scrambling Bf 109, just clearing the other Messerschmitt on take-off. A few aircraft got airborne (**2**). They banked back towards the field, strafing their earth-bound tormentors and setting several Stuarts afire. But the "tank versus parked airplane" rampage heavily favored the Americans. For half an hour Barlow's Stuarts rumbled up and down the mile-long Djedeïda airstrip with near-impunity, destroying everything in sight before withdrawing. Company C lost two killed, one tank and crew missing, and several tanks damaged, while destroying 24 Bf 109s and Ju 87s.

Thirteen miles away in Tunis, Nehring's staff was in a state of panic. But instead of pushing his reconnaissance-in-force towards Tunis, Barlow withdrew safely back to Allied lines as dusk fell. His decision wasn't second-guessed by his superiors. A rare chance to accept risk, pursue an unforeseen opportunity, and possibly upend the fragile German bridgehead had come and gone.

offensive postponed, they withdrew to Medjez el Bab under severe Luftwaffe attacks, losing 285 men. Meanwhile, No. 1 Commando came ashore west of Bizerte early on December 1, intent on linking up with a 36th Brigade Group nowhere to be found. No. 1 Commando seized their objectives and held out for three days before withdrawing, suffering 60 British and 74 American casualties. First Army held its forward lines, expecting the pause to be merely temporary. Anderson prepared CCB/1A and Blade Force to resume attacks against Tunis December 2.

By air and by sea the belligerents strove to interdict each other's supply lines. The Royal Navy re-established Malta's Force K, comprising light cruisers *Dido* and *Euryalus* and four destroyers, while at Bône on November 30, Force Q was created under Rear-Admiral Cecil Harcourt, composed of light cruisers *Aurora*, *Argonaut*, and *Sirius* and destroyers *Quentin* and *Quiberon*. In the early dark of December 2, a radarless Italian convoy unwittingly stumbled into Harcourt's lurking flotilla. Force Q opened fire from a mere 4,000 yards, quickly destroying all three Italian transports and destroyer *Folgore*. Three damaged escorts escaped. The British retired unhurt, leaving 2,200 Italian dead in their wake. At dawn, Luftwaffe torpedo bombers jumped Force Q, 50 miles from Bône, damaging *Quiberon* and sinking *Quentin*. The following night, Force K finished off a previously mauled Italian convoy of four merchantmen and a destroyer. During December, Allied air and sea action would sink a quarter of all Axis cargo dispatched to Tunisia, including 30 panzers. Axis merchantmen that ran the gauntlet were bombed in port daily by US Twelfth Air Force B-17s and B-24s, while Luftwaffe bombers struck Algiers nightly.

The crew of HMS *Argonaut* practice calisthenics while their heavily damaged vessel is docked in Algiers, in late December 1942. Operating with Force Q, the Dido-class cruiser was torpedoed on December 14 by the Italian submarine *Mocenigo*. *Argonaut* would not rejoin active service until April 1944. (IWM A 013446)

Axis counteroffensive at Tebourba, December 1

By December 1, Allied Force in Tunisia and Algeria numbered 112,860 troops; total strength in North Africa was 253,212. In contrast, 15,273 German troops and 581 tons of supplies had arrived in Tunisia by air, an average of 750 troops a day. Another 1,867 troops had come by sea, along with 159 panzers and armored cars, 127 guns, 1,097 vehicles, and 12,549 tons of supplies.

Twelfth Air Force B-17s take off to bomb Axis positions in Tunisia. This 1943 watercolor by L. S. Lee illuminates the dusty, primitive operating conditions of most Allied air bases in North Africa. The dirt strips' vulnerability to rain is apparent. (IWM LD 3981)

Despite Allied reverses, the Axis situation was desperate. Kesselring toured the front and scolded Nehring for lacking sufficient aggression. Nehring charged dynamic Generalmajor Fischer with expanding the tenuous bridgehead. Fischer scraped virtually all German manpower into four improvised *Kampfgruppen* of 64 panzers and 14 armored cars in an all-stakes gamble to repel the Allies.

Despite Ultra warnings, Fischer's December 1 counterattack perfectly spoiled Anderson's planned offensive for the following day; the Germans launched a well-coordinated,

British crewmen of a Valentine tank read letters during a respite, Tunisia, December 1942. At this point, Blade Force had been disbanded and its surviving elements dispersed to their respective parent units, leaving the US 1st Armored Division's Combat Command B as First Army's only large armored formation on the front. (IWM NA 285)

A captured Tiger in Tunisia, 1942. The Anglo-Americans encountered their first four PzKpfw VI Tiger heavy tanks on December 2, during Fischer's Tebourba counterattack. The 60-ton Tiger's thick armor and 88mm gun wildly outclassed its Allied counterparts. Thirty-one Tigers reached Tunisia before the Axis surrender in May 1943, about half by the end of 1942. (US Army)

combined-arms assault of infantry, panzers, and Stukas against Blade Force at Tebourba, just 20 miles from Tunis. Leading from the front, Fischer personally captured 15 Allied soldiers, drove them to the rear, then returned with two companies of reinforcements. Stukas operated just outside Allied artillery range and within five minutes of air support requests. In contrast, the Spitfires' 90-mile combat radius allowed five minutes over the battlefield. Airborne Stukas simply retreated out of range or landed and parked under trees until the Spitfires departed.

Blade Force suffered severe losses and Anderson dissolved the unit late on December 2. Defense of the Tebourba area was left to the 11th Brigade Group and CCB/1A. The following day, December 3, Fischer attacked again and overran 11th Brigade Group's defensive positions. The 11th Brigade Group managed to extricate itself, but a valiant defense by the 2nd Hampshires resulted in heavy casualties.

Fischer's battlegroups Lueder and Djedëida broke through and recaptured Tebourba at noon, December 4. In their haste to withdraw, 11th Brigade Group abandoned more than 400 tanks, guns, and vehicles, and over 1,000 prisoners. At El Guessa on December 6, CCB/1A suffered and inflicted heavy casualties fighting off an attack from elements of 10.Panzer-Division. Losses included the US Army's first four Sherman tanks to see action. CCB/1A and 11th Brigade Group withdrew in heavy rain that night.

Hours earlier at Souk el Khemis, Lieutenant-General C. W. Allfrey's British V Corps had assumed command of the Allied front. Under Allfrey were 78th Division, the still-arriving 6th Armoured Division, CCB/1A, 1st Parachute Brigade, and No. 1 and No. 6 Commandos.

Hitler upgraded his Tunisian formation to Army status, superseding Nehring. The new 5.Panzer-Armee was commanded by Generaloberst Hans-Jürgen von Arnim, transferred straight from the Eastern Front's Rzhev salient, where von Arnim had been commander of XXXIX Panzerkorps. Von Arnim arrived in Tunis December 8. The Tunisian force he inherited had to date been shipped 185 panzers.

Eisenhower postponed the Tunis offensive to rebuild forces, while Anderson requested to withdraw First Army to better defensive ground. Eisenhower approved December 8 with the caveat that vital areas were to be retained and Medjez el Bab held "at all costs," informing Anderson that Eisenhower "personally accepted the responsibility for any disaster" from the decision to hold Medjez el Bab. As Anderson re-formed better defensive lines, the weather covered his withdrawal and Axis interference was light. An inexplicable miscommunication sent CCB/1A's heavy equipment into impassable mud; CCB/1A eventually retrieved only three of 18 M7 105mm howitzers, 12 of 62 medium tanks, and 38 of 122 Stuart tanks.

By December 10, the Allies had been pushed back to just east of Medjez el Bab. Allied combat losses since the counterattack came to 73 tanks, 432 vehicles, 70 artillery pieces, and over 1,000 captured personnel. On December 13, von Arnim believed the immediate threat had been neutralized and reverted to the defensive.

Eisenhower disparaged Allied operations to date: "They have violated every recognized principle of war, are in conflict with all operational and logistic methods laid down in textbooks, and will be condemned in their entirety by all Leavenworth and War College classes for the next twenty-five years."

THE END OF *TORCH*

AFHQ resolved to make one last do-or-die attempt before the Tunisian rains halted the Allies for the winter. Abandoning a broad front, Eisenhower focused on simply seizing Tunis. First Army would then "crowd" the remaining Axis into northeastern Tunisia, aiming to capture Bizerte within a month of Tunis. The next several weeks the Allies rebuilt their forces, uncomfortably knowing the Axis were reinforcing as well. Time and favorable options were running out.

The Allies wielded 20,000 British, 11,000 American, and 7,000 French combat troops for their final offensive. Facing them in the Tunis bridgehead were 25,000 Axis combat troops, 10,000 support personnel, and 80 panzers. Eisenhower possessed superior artillery but the Axis would have air superiority and better (though fewer) tanks. The Allies massed their strength on a narrow, direct front to Tunis to exploit their firepower advantage. Weather and build-up issues repeatedly postponed the offensive until December 24–25.

Preceding the main offensive, Allied preliminary operations on December 22–23 would regain the Tebourba Gap approaches. The initial move demanded seizing the commanding heights of Djebel el Ahmera. This mission was assigned to the 2nd Battalion, Coldstream Guards, who would then be relieved by US 1st Battalion, 18th Infantry Regiment. Djebel el Ahmera was better known by its British moniker, "Longstop Hill."

Kesselring anticipated a new Allied offensive and funneled three infantry regiments and additional trucks to von Arnim. On December 21, German artillery observers atop Longstop Hill noticed heavy activity below, confirmed the next day by the Luftwaffe. Surprise was lost. At H-Hour, heavy rain set in and did not let up. The Allied assault began late on December 22 as the 2nd/Coldstreams wrested Longstop's summit, Hill 290, from green elements of the 754.Infanterie-Regiment. But in the nighttime downpour, 2nd/Coldstreams was inexplicably unaware of Longstop's nearby subsidiary peak,

A USAAF officer surveys his North African base, December 5, 1942. His jeep is noticeably caked in mud. All-weathering existing airfields proved unfeasible. Surfacing a single runway required 2,000 tons of steel Marston matting. The daily capacity of the Tunisian rail system servicing the entire Allied front was 950 tons. (Critical Past)

The situation in Tunisia, December 16, 1942.

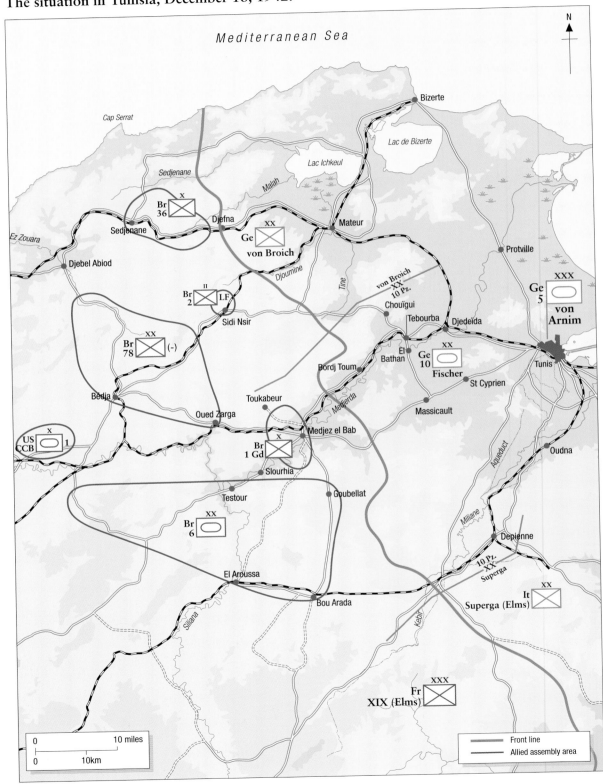

Mediterranean Sea

Cap Serrat

Bizerte

Lac de Bizerte

Lac Ichkeul

Sedjenane

Malah

Mateur

Protville

Ez Zouara

Br 36 X

Djefna

Ge von Broich XX

Djebel Abiod

Djoumine

Tine

von Broich XX 10 Pz.

Ge 5 von Arnim XXX

Br 2 LF II

Sidi Nsir

Chouïgui

Teboursa

Djedeïda

Br 78 XX (-)

Bordj Toum

El Bathan

Ge 10 Fischer XX

Tunis

Bédja

Toukabeur

Medjerda

St Cyprien

Oued Zarga

Medjez el Bab

Massicault

US CCB X 1

Br 1 Gd X

Oudna

Slourhia

Testour

Goubellat

Aqueduct

Br 6 XX

Miliane

Depienne

El Aroussa

10 Pz. XX Superga

It Superga (Elms) XX

Bou Arada

Kebil

Siliana

Fr XIX (Elms) XXX

0 ___ 10 miles
0 ___ 10km

Front line
Allied assembly area

Hill 243, still occupied by Germans, despite it being marked on maps and the Allies having occupied the area weeks earlier. Additionally, wretched visibility and mutual confusion allowed 2nd/Coldstreams and the relieving US 1st/18th Infantry to unknowingly botch the planned Longstop Hill hand-off. The reconnaissance and hand-off failures compounded each other and would prove the decisive development of the battle.

As the sun rose on December 23, the US 1st/18th Infantry discovered to their horror they only occupied half their assigned positions and German forces somehow entrenched 800 yards away. The I./69.Panzergrenadier-Regiment counterattacked and a simple hand-off of secured territory now became a fight for the US 1st/18th Infantry's survival. The initial failures, appalling weather, and German skill combined to make a shambles of the Allied operation. Taking severe casualties, British and American troops fought with great tenacity and courage in a desperate back-and-forth battle. But on December 25, the 7.Panzer-Regiment and 69.Panzergrenadier-Regiment, equally frantic, decisively drove the exhausted Anglo-Americans off the heights. The victors appropriately christened Longstop Hill *Weinachtshügel* – "Christmas Hill."

The Longstop Hill debacle had cost the Coldstream Guards 178 killed, wounded, and missing, and the Americans 356. The previous day, December 24, Eisenhower had visited V Corps headquarters and personally observed the quagmire conditions. Eisenhower reluctantly canceled the Tunis offensive for the winter. Seven weeks of unceasing, frenetic German aggression had successfully masked how frail had been the Axis toehold on Tunisia. *Torch* was officially over.

In Algiers that same afternoon, Fernand Eugene Bonnier de la Chapelle, a disturbed 20-year-old Resistance member, broke into Admiral Darlan's office with a revolver and assassinated him. Caught immediately, Chapelle was tried, convicted, and executed within two days, practically guaranteeing undying conspiracy theories.

Of Darlan's demise it was noted, "Not a tear was shed," and "Once bought, he stayed bought." Darlan's brief appearance exactly when and where he was needed, and no longer, has the appearance of a literary *deus ex machina*. However, no hard evidence of Allied scheming has ever surfaced, regarding either Darlan's timely entry or equally timely exit. The Darlan affair was simply an unusual coincidence – one the Allies badly needed and made the most of when it presented itself.

Darlan's murder left an immediate and enormous French power vacuum and only two real candidates to claim it. But Giraud hated politics and his strange personality paled alongside his charismatic rival. Darlan's assassination swept de Gaulle's path clear to assume undisputed French leadership through World War II and into the postwar period.

Forlorn-looking infantry of the 2nd Battalion, Coldstream Guards trudge across Longstop Hill at dusk, December 22–24, 1942. Heavy rain turned the ground into a muddy mess, inhibiting motorized and even mule transport. Longstop Hill was finally taken from the Germans on April 23, 1943, opening the Allied way to Tunis. (IWM NA 332)

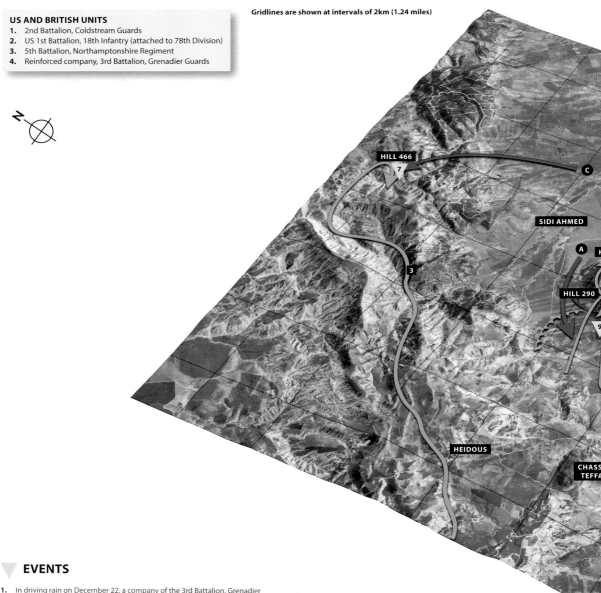

US AND BRITISH UNITS

1. 2nd Battalion, Coldstream Guards
2. US 1st Battalion, 18th Infantry (attached to 78th Division)
3. 5th Battalion, Northamptonshire Regiment
4. Reinforced company, 3rd Battalion, Grenadier Guards

HILL 466

SIDI AHMED

HILL 290

HEIDOUS

CHASS
TEFFA

▼ EVENTS

1. In driving rain on December 22, a company of the 3rd Battalion, Grenadier Guards opens the battle by occupying the village of Grich el Oued. They will be forced to withdraw December 26 as the Allied offensive collapses.

2. The 2nd Battalion, Coldstream Guards successfully assaults the stubborn but inexperienced troops of the German 754.Infanterie-Regiment atop Longstop Hill. The winter downpour will dog the Allies the next four days. The 2nd/Coldstreams secures Longstop's summit, Hill 290, but in the confusion and fading visibility they are unaware of the existence of German-held Hill 243 less than half a mile away.

3. Earlier that afternoon, the 2nd/Coldstreams' right flank overruns the railroad station Halte dëel Heri but is then expelled by a German counterattack. Believing they occupy the entire Longstop ridge above, the 2nd/Coldstreams cancels further attacks.

4. Following behind the initial attack on December 22, the US 1st Battalion, 18th Infantry Regiment departs Medjez el Bab to relieve the 2nd/Coldstreams. Miscommunication, the rainstorm, and darkness conspire to botch the overnight hand-off. The 2nd/Coldstreams, believing the 1st/18th Infantry Regiment is in control of the entire ridge, evacuates Longstop Hill at 0430hrs on December 23.

5. Dawn breaks on December 23 and 1st/18th Infantry Regiment suddenly realize they only command half the ridge. The 1st/18th Infantry Regiment's Company A advances towards Halte dëel Heri and is annihilated by a counterattacking Panzergrenadier company. The 1st/18th Infantry Regiment calls for reinforcements and the 2nd/Coldstreams are sent back to Longstop Hill.

6. 1 Battalion, 69.Panzergrenadier-Regiment drives 1st/18th Infantry Regiment off Hill 290 at 1500hrs. A 1600hrs counterattack fails to dislodge 1./69.Panzergrenadier-Regiment from Hill 290 and US 1st/18th Infantry Regiment takes defensive positions in close proximity to the Germans.

7. Meanwhile, the 5th Battalion, Northamptonshire Regiment has begun a nighttime flanking movement on December 22–23 to reach Tebourba Gap, unaware their attack has been canceled. The Germans dispatch two companies of the 754. Infanterie-Regiment to counter. In a fierce battle on the night of December 23/24, the 754.Infanterie-Regiment drive the 5th/Northamptonshires off Hill 466.

8. At 1700hrs, December 24, the 2nd/Coldstreams re-assault Longstop Hill, reclaiming Hill 290 from the Germans at dusk. Finally discovering Hill 243, they briefly win the peak, but the Germans reclaim it before dawn.

9. At 0700hrs, December 25, the Germans strike in a double envelopment: armor from the 7.Panzer-Regiment in the north and the 69.Panzergrenadier-Regiment in the south. The 69.Panzergrenadier-Regiment mauls the US 1st/18th Infantry Regiment from the rear. At 0900hrs, the Germans oust the forsaken 2nd/Coldstreams from Hill 290 and begin to tenaciously reclaim Longstop's entire ridge. The Germans are finally repulsed short of Chassart Taffaha by minefields and the 3rd/Grenadier Guards.

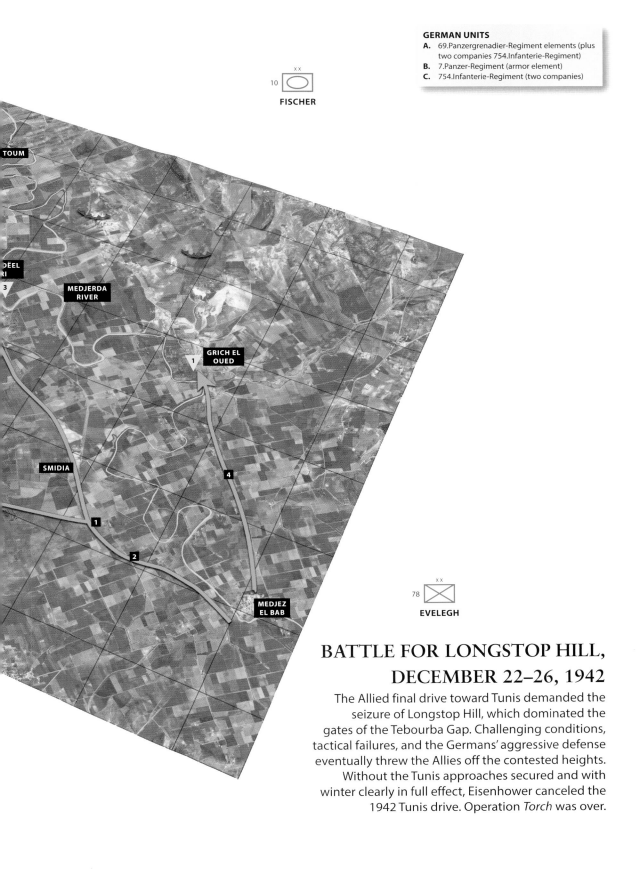

X X
10 ⬭
FISCHER

TOUM

ÖEL
RI
3

MEDJERDA
RIVER

GRICH EL
OUED
1

SMIDIA

4

1

2

MEDJEZ
EL BAB

X X
78 ⊠
EVELEGH

BATTLE FOR LONGSTOP HILL,
DECEMBER 22–26, 1942

The Allied final drive toward Tunis demanded the
seizure of Longstop Hill, which dominated the
gates of the Tebourba Gap. Challenging conditions,
tactical failures, and the Germans' aggressive defense
eventually threw the Allies off the contested heights.
Without the Tunis approaches secured and with
winter clearly in full effect, Eisenhower canceled the
1942 Tunis drive. Operation *Torch* was over.

AFTERMATH

Giraud (left) and de Gaulle (right) awkwardly shake hands for the cameras at the Casablanca Conference, January 13, 1943. The insufferably narcissistic generals thoroughly despised each other, to the smirking amusement of the seated Roosevelt (left) and Churchill (right), who insisted on the photo op. (US Army Signal Corps)

Operation *Torch* thus came to a disappointing end the final week of 1942. Major Tunisian hostilities resumed badly for the Allies in February 1943, but the ensuing post-Kasserine Pass shake-up turned the tide. Eisenhower's improved Allied Force joined Eighth Army to deliver the Axis' African coup de grace in May 1943. In completing the original *Torch* mission, Allied Force suffered 41,136 casualties, including 20,213 killed and missing; French casualties came to 16,180 with 8,100 killed and missing. Not landing deeper into the Mediterranean had proven a mistake. The Morocco landings were redundant; the pragmatic Franco had no intention of entering the war. Nevertheless, the Allies had the power to keep the Straits open.

The US Army finally claimed a major role in the European war, earning badly needed combat experience. Initially contemptuous of American soldiers, Rommel later remarked they learned war fastest. The chaotic naval battle of Casablanca taught the US Navy to decentralize amphibious command and control and adopt the Royal Navy's dedicated "command" transport rather than coordinate landings from a warship. Three glaring errors of *Torch* were

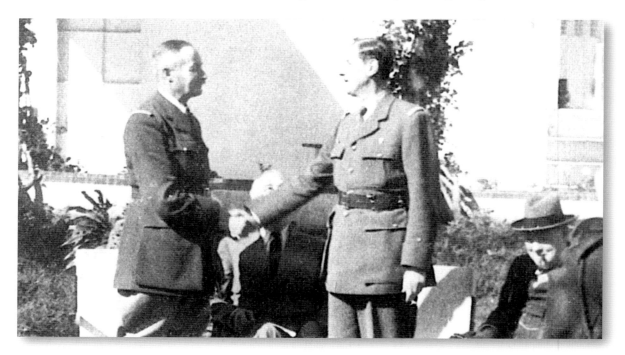

the *Terminal* and *Reservist* raids and the *Villain* airborne drop. That all three failed without affecting the success of *Torch* reveals their irrelevance. One notices *Overlord* included no operation so contrived.

Operation *Torch* inaugurated a substantial new drain on Germany's Eastern Front, dealing material consequences to the Wehrmacht. Admittedly, separating the strategic effects of *Torch* from Eighth Army can be difficult, but between November 1942 and May 1943 the Germans lost 2,422 aircraft in the Mediterranean Theater, or 40 percent of the Luftwaffe's November 1942 strength. This includes over 1,000 fighters and 900 bombers. The transport fleet was heavily affected. By December 1942, 320 Ju 52s had been rushed to North Africa – just when they were so badly needed at Stalingrad. By January 1943, the Luftwaffe had lost 164 Ju 52s in North Africa (14 percent of its fleet). Combined with the Stalingrad debacle, the Luftwaffe lost 659 transports (56 percent of November's fleet). Confronted with the urgent and unexpected Tunisian airlift, the Luftwaffe was forced to raid its own training establishment for pilots. By mid-1943, scores of priceless German flight instructors had been slaughtered over the Mediterranean by Allied fighters. Its flight schools decimated, the Luftwaffe creeped closer to 1944's catastrophic death spiral.

The Heer also lost critical resources to *Torch*. Between November 1942 and May 1943, the Wehrmacht shipped 510 panzers to North Africa. All were lost when von Arnim's and Rommel's armies were destroyed – one-sixth of the period's panzer production and equivalent to one-fifth Eastern Front strength. Hitler's decision to reinforce Tunisia frustrated an early Allied theater victory but resulted in the bagging of 238,000 Axis personnel in May 1943, comparable to Stalingrad in material scale.

Proud, tired, and relieved, US troops mill around Casablanca immediately after the armistice. Operation *Torch* was among the boldest, most complex offensives of World War II and despite its flaws, it achieved complete strategic surprise. (Photo by Albert Harlingue/ Roger Viollet/Getty Images)

With North Africa secure, Britain reasserted control over the Mediterranean. Malta's long, tenuous ordeal to survive abruptly ended. The shorter Suez convoy route vis-a-vis Cape Horn demanded only 25 percent of previous shipping; strategic implications were immediate. Eventually knocking Italy out of the war proved hollow; after September 1943, the Germans tenaciously defended the rugged peninsula, tying down more Allied power than the reverse. Italy provided a useful base for the USAAF Fifteenth Air Force's strategic bombing of the Reich but otherwise proved a strategic dead end.

Torch mercifully killed the preposterous *Sledgehammer*, which the British correctly recognized had disaster written all over it. The Americans' theatrical reaction to *Sledgehammer*'s rejection belies their claims that the invasion plan was merely a "contingency" operation. More compelling is *Roundup*. *Roundup* had significant logistic and planning issues to resolve in just eight months, but so did *Overlord* a year later. *Roundup*'s biggest weakness was always the idea of throwing a virtually untested US Army onto the Continent against the Wehrmacht. Yet Hitler's "Atlantic Wall" was far weaker in 1943. Did *Torch* unnecessarily prolong the European war? American acquiescence to *Torch* permanently altered the Western Allies' strategic course in World War II. There would be no invasion of mainland Europe in 1943. As Roosevelt's staff had feared, the success of *Torch* meant American military power would increasingly get sucked into the indecisive Mediterranean Theater. Despite "Europe first," by September 1943 the United States posted 361,000 personnel in Britain, but 610,000 in the Mediterranean and over 700,000 in Asia and the Pacific. The invasion of mainland Europe would not be seriously revisited until May 1943 and not be firmly agreed to until the Tehran Conference in November. But if the Americans had been wrong about *Sledgehammer*, the Third Reich's 1945 *Götterdämmerung* proved overall American strategy frightfully correct – in hindsight no British-style peripheral war could ever have destroyed Nazi Germany.

Before *Torch*, the "special relationship" between Britain and the United States did not exist. The extraordinary cooperation of *Torch* overcame mutual suspicions and inaugurated one of history's most successful wartime alliances. The unassuming Eisenhower became destined almost by default to become the ETO's supreme commander. As each campaign concluded successfully, arbitrarily replacing Eisenhower with someone less proven grew increasingly unlikely.

The last word belongs with *Torch*'s most enduring and enthusiastic proponent. At a London dinner on November 10, 1942, a triumphant Churchill spoke glowingly of El Alamein and *Torch*. Addressing the extraordinary North African events of recent days, Churchill mused, "Now this is not the end. It is not even the beginning of the end. But it is, perhaps, the end of the beginning."

THE BATTLEFIELDS TODAY

The global decolonization movement swept North Africa after 1945. Morocco and Tunisia would win their independence from France relatively bloodlessly by 1956. Algeria was a different matter, emerging sovereign in 1962 only after a long, bitter civil war that claimed over 200,000 dead. The new Islamic socialist governments virtually eliminated the native European and Jewish populations by inspiring their mass exodus to metropolitan France. The revolutions therefore permanently altered the cultural and demographic character of the region.

Some relics of *Torch* survive. Now Kenitra, Port Lyautey's airfield became a major US Navy airbase until 1991; it remains an active facility of the Royal Moroccan Air Force. The Kasbah was rebuilt after 1942 and still looms over the Sebou. Numerous Moroccan bunkers survive, while Hotel Miramar, Patton's Fedala headquarters, is still in business. A few American companies host tours of the Moroccan *Torch* battlefields. For Casablanca, Oran, and Algiers, *Torch* remains a mere blip on their rich, centuries-long histories. Rugged Tunisian battlefields such as Longstop Hill remain largely undeveloped. World War II monuments and cemeteries dot North Africa; less than a mile from ancient Carthage rest 2,841 Americans who died in the 1942–43 North African campaign, including 240 unknowns.

Fortunately, two American battleships that took part in *Torch* have been preserved: *Texas* at San Jacinto State Park near Houston and *Massachusetts* at Fall River's Battleship Cove, both in their namesake states. *Texas* is the world's only surviving World War I dreadnought and *Massachusetts* still retains her scar from El Hank's single shell hit off Casablanca. Both battleships are open to the public as the flagship attractions of larger military history parks.

ACRONYMS AND ABBREVIATIONS

AAS	Antiaircraft auxiliary
ACV	Auxiliary carrier
AFHQ	Allied Force Headquarters, North Africa
AMT	Auxiliary minesweeper
AK	Cargo ship
AO	Fleet oiler
AP	Transport
APA	Attack transport
AT	Ocean tug

BB	Battleship
BM	Monitor
BLT	Battalion Landing Team
CA	Heavy cruiser
CC	Battlecruiser
CL	Light cruiser
CM	Large minesweeper
CV	Aircraft carrier
CVE	Escort carrier
CVL	Light carrier
DCA	Défense contre Avions (antiaircraft)
DD	Destroyer
DS	Sloop
DC	Corvette
DE	Frigate
DMS	High-speed minesweeper
ETOUSA	European Theater of Operations, US Army
FG	Fighter group
GACA	Groupe Autonome de Chasseurs d'Afrique (African Chasseurs Mobile Squadron Group)
GB	Groupe de Bombardement (Bomber Group)
GC	Groupe de Chasse (Fighter Group)
GR	Groupe de Reconnaissance (Reconnaissance Group)
GT	Groupe de Transport (Transport Group)
LSG	Landing ship gantry
LSH	Landing ship headquarters
LSI(H)	Landing ship infantry (hand-hoisting)
LSI(L)	Landing ship infantry (large)
LSI(M)	Landing ship infantry (medium)
LST	Landing ship tank
OB	Oberbefehlshaber
OSS	Office of Strategic Services
PB	Patrol boat
PIR	Parachute Infantry Regiment
PT	Torpedo boat
RA	Régiment d'Artillerie (Artillery Regiment)
RAA	Régiment d'Artillerie d'Afrique (African Artillery Regiment)
RACM	Régiment d'Artillerie Coloniale du Maroc (Moroccan Colonial Artillery Regiment)
RAF	Royal Air Force
RCA	Régiment de Chasseurs d'Afrique (African Chasseurs Regiment)
RCT	Regimental Combat Team
REC	Régiment Étranger de Cavalerie (Foreign Legion Cavalry Regiment)
REI	Régiment Étranger d'Infanterie (Foreign Legion Infantry Regiment)
RG	Régiment de la Garde (Guard Regiment)
RIC	Régiment d'Infanterie Coloniale (Colonial Infantry Regiment)
RICM	Régiment d'Infanterie Coloniale du Maroc (Mixed Colonial Infantry Regiment)
RLG	Regimental Landing Group
RMZT	Régiment Mixte de Zouaves et Tirailleurs (Mixed Colonial and Zouaves Infantry Regiment)

RN	Royal Navy
RSA	Régiment de Spahis Algériens (Algerian Spahis Regiment)
RSM	Régiment de Spahis Marocains (Moroccan Spahis Regiment)
RST	Régiment de Spahis Tunisiens (Tunisian Spahis Regiment)
RTA	Régiment de Tirailleurs Algériens (Algerian Rifle Regiment)
RTM	Régiment de Tirailleurs Marocains (Moroccan Rifle Regiment)
RTS	Régiment de Tirailleurs Sénégalais (Senegalese Rifle Regiment)
RTT	Régiment de Tirailleurs Tunisiens (Tunisian Rifle Regiment)
RZ	Régiment de Zouaves (Zouaves Regiment)
SA	Sapeurs Annamites (Annamite Sappers)
USAAF	US Army Air Forces
USN	US Navy

SELECT BIBLIOGRAPHY

Reports

Anderson, Kenneth, *Report of the Commander-in-chief First Army to the Secretary of State for War, 8th November 1942–13th May 1943* (1943)

Cunningham, Andrew, *Report of Operation "Torch" Proceedings from the Commander-in-Chief Mediterranean to the Commander-in-Chief Allied Forces, 30th March, 1943* (1943)

Eisenhower, Dwight D., *Report of the Commander-in-Chief Allied Forces to the Combined Chiefs of Staff on Operations in Northwest Africa* (1943)

Hull, R. A., *War Diary of Blade Force, 13 Nov. '42 to 12 Dec. '42* (1943)

Official/semi-official histories

Beck, Alfred M., Bortz, Abe, Lynch, Charles W., Mayo, Lida and Weld, Ralph F., *The Corps of Engineers: The War Against Germany*, US Army Center for Military History, 1985

Bykofsky, Joseph and Larson, Harold *The Transportation Corps: Operations Overseas*, US Army Center for Military History, 1957

Caroff, Rene, *Les Débarquements alliés en Afrique du Nord (Novembre 1942)*, Service historique de la Marine, 1987

Cline, Ray S. ,*Washington Command Post: The Operations Division*, The War Department, 1951

Craven, W. F. and Cate, J. L. (eds.), *Army Air Forces in World War II*, Volume II: *Europe: TORCH to POINTBLANK August 1942 to December 1943*, Office of Air Force History, 1983

Historical Section, COMNAVEU, *Administrative History of U.S. Naval Forces in Europe, 1940–1946*, Volume V: *The Invasion of Normandy: Operation NEPTUNE*, Navy Department, 1946

Howe, George F., *Northwest Africa: Seizing the Initiative in the West*; United States Army in World War II: *Mediterranean Theater of Operations*, US Army Center for Military History, 1957

Leighton, Richard M. and Coakley, Robert W., *Global Logistics and Strategy, 1940–1943*, US Army Center for Military History, 1955

Longo, Luigi Emilio, *Giovanni Messe: l'ultimo maresciallo d'Italia*, Stato maggiore dell'esercito, Ufficio storico, 2006

Meyer, Leo J., "The Decision to Invade North Africa'" Chapter 7 in Greenfield, Kent Roberts (ed.), *Command Decisions*, US Army Center for Military History, 1960

Morison, Samuel E. *Operations in North African Waters, October 1942–June 1943: History of United States Naval Operations in World War II*, Naval Institute Press, 2010

Playfair, I. S. O., *The Mediterranean and Middle East*, Volume IV: *The Destruction of Axis Forces in Africa*, HMSO, 1966

Richards, Denis and Saunders, Hilary St. G., *Royal Air Force 1939–1945*, Volume II: *The Fight Avails*, HMSO, 1954

Roskill, S. W., *The War at Sea 1939–1945*, Volume II: *The Period of Balance*, HMSO, 1956

United States Army Air Forces, *The AAF in Northwest Africa*, Center for Air Force History, 1945

Articles/essays

Arthy, Andrew, *The American Tank Raid on Djedeida Airfield, 25 November 1942*, 2004

Daubin, Freeland A., Jr, *The Battle for Happy Valley*, US Army, 1948

Mersky, Peter, "Naval Aviation in Operation Torch," *Naval Aviation News,*
    November–December 1992
Murray, Williamson, *Strategy for Defeat: The Luftwaffe 1933–1945,* Air University Press, 1983
Books
Atkinson, Rick, *An Army at Dawn: The War in North Africa, 1942–1943,* Abacus, 2003
Breuer, William B., *Operation Torch: The Allied Gamble to Invade North Africa,*
    St Martin's Press, 1985
Gildea, Robert, *Fighters in the Shadows: A New History of the French Resistance,* Faber and
    Faber Ltd., 2015
O'Hara, Vincent P., *Torch: North Africa and the Allied Path to Victory,* Naval Institute Press, 2015
Roberts, Andrew, *Masters and Commanders: How Four Titans Won the War in the West,*
    1941–1945, Harper Perennial, 2010
Rottman, Gordon, *US World War II Amphibious Tactics: Mediterranean and European*
    Theaters, Osprey Publishing Ltd., 2006
Sumner, Ian and Vauvillier, François, *The French Army 1939-45 (1),* Osprey Publishing Ltd., 1998
Websites
france1940.free.fr/en_index.html
www.captainwalker.uk
www.combinedops.com
www.navsource.org
www.niehorster.org
www.ibiblio.org/hyperwar
www.ww2survivorstories.com
www.ww2db.com

INDEX

Figures in **bold** refer to illustrations.